# Wild About Weather

# Wild About Weather

## 50 Wet, Windy & Wonderful Activities

ED BROTAK

LARK BOOKS

A Division of Sterling Publishing Co., Inc.
New York

## Dedication

I would like to dedicate this book to my wife, Liz, and my two daughters, Chandler and Brayton. Even weather fanatics need some balance in their lives.

editor
**Joe Rhatigan**

associate editor
**Veronika Alice Gunter**

art director
**Susan McBride**

associate art director
**Shannon Yokeley**

cover design
**Barbara Zaretsky**

editorial assistance
**Delores Gosnell**

production assistance
**Melanie Cooper**

photography
**Keith Wright**
**keithwright.com**

illustrations
**Orrin Lundgren**
**Susan McBride**

The Library of Congress has cataloged the hardcover edition as follows:

Brotak, Ed.
  Wild about weather : 50 wet, windy & wonderful activities / by Ed Brotak.
    p. cm.
  Includes index.
  ISBN 1-57990-468-8
  1. Weather—Juvenile literature. 2. Weather—Experiments—Juvenile literature. I. Title.
QC981.3.B745 2004
551.6'078—dc22

                                        2004004988


10 9 8 7 6 5 4 3 2 1

Published by Lark Books, A Division of
Sterling Publishing Co., Inc.
387 Park Avenue South, New York, N.Y. 10016

First Paperback Edition 2005
Text © 2004, Ed Brotak
Photography (except as noted), illustrations, & project designs © 2004, Lark Books

Distributed in Canada by Sterling Publishing,
c/o Canadian Manda Group, 165 Dufferin Street
Toronto, Ontario, Canada M6K 3H6

Distributed in the U.K. by Guild of Master Craftsman Publications Ltd.,
Castle Place, 166 High Street, Lewes, East Sussex, England, BN7 1XU
Tel: (+ 44) 1273 477374, Fax: (+ 44) 1273 478606, Email:
pubs@thegmcgroup.com, Web: www.gmcpublications.com

Distributed in Australia by Capricorn Link (Australia) Pty Ltd.,
P.O. Box 704, Windsor, NSW 2756 Australia

If you have questions or comments about this book,
please contact:
Lark Books
67 Broadway
Asheville, NC 28801
(828) 253-0467

Manufactured in China

ISBN 1-57990-468-8 (hardcover) 1-57990-749-0 (paperback)

For information about custom editions, special sales, premium and corporate purchases, please contact Sterling Special Sales Department at 800-805-5489 or specialsales@sterlingpub.com.

## Photo Credits

**Grant Goodge:** 6 (center), 7 (center & right), 8, 9, 24, 36, 39 (left), 44 (right), 52 (upper & lower right), 61, 68, 72, 73, 76, 82, 83, 84, 85, 87, 88, 89, 91, 93 (upper left & lower right), 95, 100, 101, 108 (bottom), 116, 122 (bottom)

**NOAA:** 19 (lower left), 39 (center & right), 44, 47 (left), 111, 122 (top and middle)

**Brand X Pictures:** 18

**Weatherstock:** front cover, 5, 6 (right), 7 (left), 10, 14 (center & right), 16, 17,19 (center). 20, 21, 23, 37 (center), 38, 47 (center & right), 52 (upper & lower left), 54, 60, 71, 77, 81, 93 (lower left & upper right), 97, 98, 103, 105, 106, 108 (top), 109, 112, 119

**Photodisc:** 26, 41, 44 (left), 113

## Acknowledgments

I'd like to thank the staff at Lark Books for all their help on this project. In particular, I want to thank my editor, Joe Rhatigan, for his constant encouragement and for his expertise in guiding me along in this, my first book. I also wish to thank fellow weather fanatic Grant Goodge for his spectacular weather photos that grace this book.

Special thanks also go out to Susan McBride, Veronika Gunter, Keith Wright, and all the kids who modeled for this book, including Bailey Boyd, Barcley Boyd, Anna Weshner-Dunning, Tobie Weshner, Allen Mitchiner, Jr., Alex Mitchiner, Chandler Brotak, Anna Costa, Rabb Scott, Tye V. Smarjesse, Camille Rae Smarjesse, Kayleigh Rhatigan, Sam Scott, Jake Buske, and Zoe Jackson. Thanks Weather Mom (Megan Kirby) and Weather Dad (Jason Thompson).

# Contents

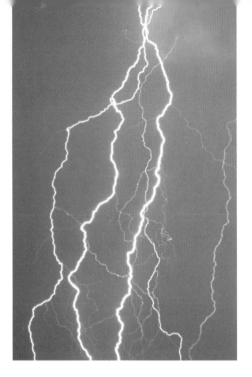

# Introduction

Hi! I'm Dr. Ed, and I am a **Weather Fanatic.**

**W**eather Fanatics are people who love the weather. Most of us can't remember not being interested in the weather; it's like we were born this way. We track storms and spend hours on the Internet at all the weather sites. We can name everyone on The Weather Channel. Most of us keep weather records at our homes.

When I decided I wanted to make a living doing the weather, I went to college and got a degree in *meteorology*, the study of weather. Actually, I got a bunch of degrees. For the past 25 years, I've been teaching weather to college students.

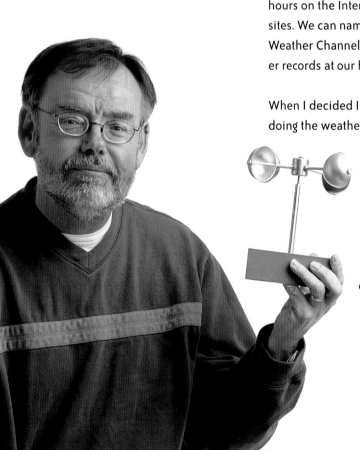
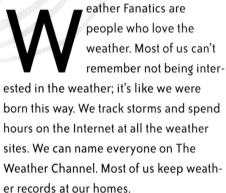

Some of my students are just regular people who want to know more about the weather. Some are Weather Fanatics like me and want to have careers in weather. I've taught thousands of students over the years and a few hundred have gone on in meteorology. Some have jobs with the government, some work for private companies, and some are even on television.

I love explaining the weather to people, and that's why I've written this book. So, whether you're a Weather Fanatic in training or simply someone who wants answers to your weather questions, this book is for you.

# What's in This Book

**Although weather is often chaotic,** I've tried to give this book a logical order.

**Chapter 1:** In this chapter, you'll tune into the weather information that's all around you, travel back in time and figure out why weather was often a matter of life and death, and prepare to make your very first weather forecast.

**Chapter 2:** Fasten your seatbelts and get ready to explore our atmosphere, where all of our weather happens.

**Chapter 3:** You'll check out how the Sun heats things up, why we have seasons, and why, thankfully, we don't freeze to death every night.

**Chapter 4:** You'll explore not only what causes wind, but also what the wind brings with it. You'll also see how winds, large and small, fit into the whole weather picture.

**Chapter 5:** In this chapter, you'll figure out how and why humidity can affect us so much, and you'll also create some fun instruments that can measure how much water vapor is in the air, and how that will affect the weather.

**Chapter 6:** Meet the clouds and create your very own. Collect some rain, and yes, make some of your very own. Want snow? Well, you'll have to figure out how to predict some. I'll help.

**Chapter 7:** You'll learn everything you wanted to know about thunderstorms, tornadoes, and hurricanes—the most destructive forces of nature out there. You'll also get a chance to make some lightning, and become a hurricane tracker.

**Chapter 8:** Now you have all the tools you need to forecast your own weather. Put together your weather station, decipher some weather maps, and go ahead, forecast some rain for tomorrow. Or will it snow? Sunshine, you say? It's your call.

**In each chapter, you'll find cool projects and activities,** interesting facts that will impress friends, and Weather Stations, which are helpful hints for becoming the go-to guy or gal whenever someone wants to know what the weather will be like tomorrow. My forecast for today, tomorrow, and beyond: you'll have a great time exploring this book.

*"Everybody talks about the weather, but nobody does anything about it."*

—Mark Twain

9

# CHAPTER 1

# Hello Weather!

**Y**ou've experienced weather since the day you were born, but now it's time for a formal introduction.

Weather is the state of the *atmosphere* (which is the air all around you), or, in other words, what it's doing outside. And, it's always doing something outside. Even on those fair and sunny days, things are happening. You just can't see them. And then there are days when the weather is a lot more obvious. You can feel the wind blowing, see the clouds moving in, and touch the rain or snow. The next thing you know, you're in the middle of a storm. Cool! So, say "Hi" to the weather, shake its hand, and keep reading.

# A Day in the Life of You & the Weather

We spend a lot of time inside: inside our homes, our schools, the mall, or a car or bus that takes us to those and other inside places. Sometimes, it's easy to forget about the weather that's outside. Better not, though. The weather affects how you dress, how you feel, what you eat, where you go on vacation, and even why you live where you do. Check it out!

## Breakfast

Your mom is reading the newspaper at the breakfast table. She says, "They're predicting an El Niño this winter. That could mean lots of storms." Your dad, who's a building contractor, replies, "That could really slow down our project." You just smile, thinking about canceled school and snowball fights.

## Getting Ready for School

"Honey," your mom says, "the weather on the radio said it's cold and rainy this morning. Wear your heavy jacket, and bring an umbrella." You don't bring either. You're going to be inside today.

## At the Bus Stop

There's a heavy blanket of clouds overhead. You notice that you feel sort of down. So does everyone else at the bus stop. It's more quiet than usual. At first, you feel fine, and can't wait to go home and tell your mom that it wasn't cold out. Then it starts to rain. Now, you're wet and cold. You're thinking, "Why didn't somebody tell me the weather was going to be like this?" Okay, somebody did.

## On the Bus

It's raining, so the bus driver goes extra slow. She says she knew it was going to rain today when her knee started hurting last night. How'd she do that? You get to school late and have to hustle to your first class.

## History Class

You're learning about a war between England and Spain hundreds of years ago. England won the war because a huge storm sank the Spanish armada of ships.

## Science Class

You're studying rain forests. They're found near the equator. Your science teacher says that's because it's always hot and wet in those regions.

## Language Arts

Your essay on how Hurricane Isabel ruined your summer vacation at the coast got a B+. You spelled "hurricane" wrong.

## Lunchtime

That hamburger you're eating was once a cow that ate some hay that couldn't grow without rain and sun. And the water in that soda you're drinking was originally in the sky. (Okay, maybe you're eating healthier than that, but you get the picture.)

## Math Class

In math class, you're working on simple equations, such as converting Fahrenheit temperatures into Celsius and vice versa. How come everybody doesn't use the same temperature scale?

Mom was right, I'm freezing and wet!

## On the Bus Line

The rain is miraculously gone. The sun is out, and everybody's buzzing away, waiting to get on the buses. It's not just the end of the day kind of happiness, but it's also the weather. It's warm and sunny, and everyone is feeling better. Turned out to be an okay day after all.

Yeah, I'm cool.

## I DIDN'T KNOW THAT!

There's scientific proof that sunshine can be essential to mood. Researchers have identified something called *Seasonal Affective Disorder*, a state of depression caused by a biochemical imbalance due to a lack of sunlight and shorter days during the winter months. The main treatment? Daily doses of bright light from a powerful lightbulb. This could be helpful for rainy days, but essential for people living in places with very few daylight hours, such as Barrow, Alaska, where the sun sets in late November each year and doesn't rise again until late January.

13

# Weather Information Everywhere!

**We rely on TV, newspapers, Internet sites, and radio to tell us whether or not our Semi-Annual Potato Sack Race on Saturday is going to be rained out. Is any one source more accurate than another?**

## WHAT YOU NEED

Paper and pencil

Chart on page 125

Use of a photocopier (optional)

Daily newspaper

Radio

Use of an Internet-connected computer

Television

## WHAT YOU DO

**1** Create a chart like the one on page 125, or photocopy the chart.

**2** Make a list of all the sources of local weather information you can find. Check out your hometown newspaper, listen to local radio stations, check out the Internet, and watch your local TV news and national weather cable station. You can even ask a Weather Fanatic for his or her opinion.

**3** Using the chart, keep track of the forecasts given by each source. Answer some of these questions: Which sources provide the most information? Which cover national weather as well? How do they compare?

**4** The next day, check the weather that was predicted by the sources. Which source was the most accurate? Was any source flat-out wrong?

# Check out the Weather for Yourself

**People have been observing the weather for as long as there have been people. And they didn't always have instruments— just their own senses. You can be a weather observer, too, and all you really need are your five senses.**

## WHAT YOU NEED

Pencil and paper

Internet access (optional)

## WHAT YOU DO

**1** Go outside.

**2** Answer these questions: Does it feel warm or cold? Is it damp or dry? Is the sky clear, partly cloudy, or overcast? Is it raining or snowing? Is the wind blowing? Write down what you observe.

**3** Also write down how you feel about the weather—good or bad. Different people like different things about the weather.

**4** If you want, you can check out your local weather in the U.S., by going to **http://www.weather.gov**. There you'll see a map of the United States, with highlights of significant weather. Find where you live on the map and use the mouse to click on that spot. This will take you to the website of the National Weather Service Office that serves your area. Click on anything you want to see. Don't worry if you don't understand all of the weather information at this point. I'll explain things as we go along.

**5** To check out your local weather in Canada, go to **http://weatheroffice.ec.gc.ca/canada_e.html**. There you'll see a map of Canada. Find where you live on the map and use the mouse to click on that spot. This will take you to the website of the Canadian Weather Service Office that serves your area. Click on anything you want to see.

# Weather & the Supernatural

**M**agic hammers make thunder. A man floating on a chair in the sky hurls lightning bolts. And dragons exhale clouds, then breathe fire on them, to make rain.

These may sound like spooky bedtime stories to you; however, thousands (or even just hundreds) of years ago these were real weather reports. That's right—long before weather forecasters could check their computers to see whether it was going to rain the next day (long before meteorology as well as most of the other sciences were even invented), our ancestors used stories to explain the often scary weather they witnessed outside.

Weather is so important, yet so uncontrollable, that people were convinced that powers greater than nature—maybe divine or miraculous—controlled the wind, rain, sun, and more. So that's where the Norse god Thor, Greek god Zeus, and Chinese divine dragons came from. Untrained "meteorologists" created these stories to explain the local weather. This is what people thought when lightning struck the village: "Oh, no! The gods are angry with us! We'd better be extra good."

## Rituals

But that's not all. This belief that gods or supernatural animals controlled the weather led to the practice of weather rituals, or ceremonies. Why? Hey, if you can do a dance to make the gods happy, you'll get the weather you want; and if you get the weather you want, your crops won't die, the rivers will flow, and everybody will live happily ever after. These rituals entertained people and showed respect for the supernatural forces.

## Some Rain Rituals

● Hopi people of North America created dances to perform while praying for rain. They based one dance on the movements of buffalo, the main source of food and materials for most everything Hopis made and used.

● People in western Inner Mongolia built stone monuments, festooned them with silk banners, and then sprinkled the site with milk and water while praying and burning incense.

● In Zimbabwe, rain dances ranged from short, simple ones performed by a family in front of their home to hours-long rituals, in which some people went into a trance, possessed by the rain-making spirit.

● Taoists in the Orient offered sacrifices to bring rain, a practice that could include ritual breathing, pacing, burning a talisman (charm) on an altar, and fasting.

● Mayans offered different sacrifices, including beheading dogs, chickens, and even people at the top of elaborate temples, all to gain the favor of the rain god, Chac.

Think you're way too smart to believe in superstitious weather rituals anymore? Ever sing, "Rain, rain, go away…" during a rainstorm? Are you even just a teensy bit afraid of thunder? And what's up with that groundhog on page 19 anyway? Hmm…

# WEATHER CHALLENGE:
## THE WONDERFUL & WACKY
# Weather Idiom* Quiz

**RAINING CATS AND DOGS TODAY?** Well, get your head out of the clouds, grab a fair-weather friend, and get ready to take the world by storm with this fun quiz that proves that weather is everywhere—even in things we say every day. Simply match the idiom with what it really means. The answers are at the bottom of the page.

### Weather Cliché

1. Full of hot air
2. Fair-weather friend
3. Got your head in the clouds
4. Take the world by storm
5. An ill wind blows
6. Darkest before the dawn
7. On cloud nine
8. A snowball's chance in hell
9. Under the weather
10. Rain or shine
11. Weather the storm
12. Run like the wind
13. Sail into the sunset
14. Skating on thin ice
15. The sky's the limit
16. Throw caution to the wind
17. Every cloud has a silver lining
18. When it rains, it pours
19. Don't rain on my parade
20. Take the wind out of your sails

### What It Means

A. Bad times are ahead
B. To leave happily for good
C. To persevere through hard times
D. To discourage or stop someone
E. To go quickly
F. Nothing is as bad as it seems
G. When someone talks on and on about something he knows nothing about
H. Don't spoil my good time
I. Spaced out
J. Feeling sick
K. To take a risk
L. Just when things couldn't get any worse, they tend to get better
M. Someone who sticks around only when times are good
N. When things are bad, they're really bad
O. You're about to get yourself in trouble
P. It will happen no matter what the circumstances are
Q. Unlikely…really, really unlikely
R. To become quickly famous and popular
S. You can accomplish anything
T. To feel great about a personal success

\* An idiom is an expression that uses common words and phrases out of context. In other words, when you say, "Please don't rain on my parade," you're not worried about your marching band getting wet. You're actually telling someone to stop ruining your good time.

# Weather Lore

Keeping track of the weather is one thing, but forecasting it is something else. In ancient days (before there were computers), some people tried relating things they observed to changes in the weather. Over the years, this developed into "weather lore." For example: Red sky in morning, sailor take warning. Red sky at night, sailor's delight.

This weather saying has been around for thousands of years. Does it work?

"Red sky in morning" means it's fairly clear to the east, where the sun is rising. Does that mean there are storms clouds to the west? Sometimes. "Red sky at night" means the sky is red to the west, where the sun went down. Red skies occur only when few, if any, clouds are present, and, because weather usually moves from west to east, that should mean fair weather for a while.

ASK THE EXPERT

So, you think that in the age of technology we have no more weather myths? How about Groundhog Day? Legend has it that if a groundhog sees its shadow on February 2, then six more weeks of winter are coming. If not, winter will be over soon. Does it work? What do you think?

**Q**: How come some people can "feel" the weather—for example, the bus driver who knows it will rain because her knee hurts?

**A**: Air pressure (see page 26) can effect the fluids in our bodies, and, theoretically, that can affect how our bodies function. In some countries, the theory has reached mainstream acceptance: Germany issues a daily report of how the weather might affect your health, called "Biowetter." It covers dozens of medical conditions, from arthritis pain to migraines, and rates the weather's ability to aggravate each condition.

# Create a Weather Log

Using the chart on page 126, you can start your own weather log. Fill in all the information you can from local weather forecasts or from your own observations. You won't understand all the information at this point, but whenever you get to a Weather Station, you'll be able to fill in another piece of the weather puzzle.

## WHAT YOU NEED

Log chart (see page 126)
Pencil
Use of a photocopier
Paper hole punch
Binder

## WHAT YOU DO

**1** Keep watching the weather, following the activity on page 15.

**2** Make several copies of the Log Chart on page 126. Use the hole punch to create holes so the pages fit in the binder.

**3** Date each Log Chart page, and fill in the current day's information.

**4** As you read this book and keep track of your observations and predictions, you may find that as time passes your predictions get better and better. Keep reading!

WEATHER FANATIC WARNING: WEATHER WATCHING CAN BE HABIT FORMING!

# Your First Forecast

Simply keeping a weather log for a week or two will often give you enough information to start looking for patterns. Each Weather Station in this book will show you how to predict another aspect of weather, so keep working on your weather log, and stay tuned!

## So, How Do Forecasters Predict the Weather, Anyway?

Forecasting the weather is an art and a science. Good forecasters not only know some meteorology, but they also have lots of experience watching the weather so they can often make educated guesses .

To start with, forecasters must know as much as possible about what's happening right now. Anything they miss can come back and bite them later. So they take weather observations; they record what's going on now, such as the temperature, humidity, winds, pressure, and current weather. A lot of this is done today by automated stations, not people. There are hundreds of these stations across the United States and thousands around the world. Keep in mind that we also need to know what's going on above us. Twice a day, government meteorologists send up radiosondes, which are weather instruments taken up by balloons at hundreds of stations around the world. Throw in radar and satellite data and you've got a reasonable idea of what's going on now.

Back in the old days (before 1960), all meteorologists had to go on to make a forecast was current data (what's happening right now), past trends, and their own knowledge and intuition. It was fun, but not all that accurate. Today's weather forecasts are produced mainly by computers. Fortunately for us meteorologists, computer forecasts aren't perfect. So, we get to keep our jobs.

## Dr. Ed, FORECASTER

Even though I am a teacher and not a forecaster, I am often asked to forecast the weather. At a graduation ceremony at a college I once taught at, I was asked whether the thunderstorms that were predicted for that day would hold off until after the ceremony, which was set for 10:30 a.m. to 12:00 p.m. I said to go for it but keep it moving. I recall listening to all the speakers, wishing they would hurry up. Finally, the last person marched out right at 12:00 p.m. At 12:01 p.m. (no kidding), there was a burst of thunder and a flood of rain. Am I always this good? Well, let's just say that once at the same school, I guaranteed my colleagues that the snowstorm that was fast approaching would quickly change to rain. The next morning, I couldn't see my car. It was buried under a 5-foot snowdrift.

# Recipe for Weather

**Wash your hands, put on your apron and hit the kitchen for this fun recipe… Okay, this isn't a real recipe, but it will help you figure out what's in the rest of this book.**

## INGREDIENTS

Air pressure

Sun

Wind

Humidity/precipitation

## INSTRUCTIONS

**1** Combine all your ingredients in the atmosphere. Blend well. Tah-da! You've got weather! That was easy, wasn't it!?

**Serves: All of Earth**

**TRUE OR FALSE?**
If the woolly bear caterpillar has a wide brown band, the winter will be mild. If the black band is wide, it'll be cold.

**False:** No one has ever proved this to be true.

# CHAPTER 2
# Under Pressure

**Y**OU may not feel it or see it, but there's a lot more to air than you think!

You can't have weather without air. Actually, come to think about it, you can't have anything without air. Yes, air is good stuff. When we breathe, we're taking in air. All animals do. Plants take in air, too. Plants and animals also need water. That water comes from the air. You can't have fire without air. Think about that on a cold day. In fact, the air holds in some of the Sun's heat. But, at the same time, the air blocks some of the harmful rays of the Sun and destroys most meteoroids before they can hit the Earth's surface. The air is also a perfect place to start when looking at the weather, because weather is what's going on in the air. In fact, air is heavy stuff! And the weight of the air around us can actually tell us whether there'll be clear skies or clouds and precipitation ahead. Like I said, that air is good stuff!

# Fasten Your Seatbelts

Have you ever flown in a plane? If you have, you've been up in the air. At times, it can get pretty bumpy up there and the pilot will put on the "Fasten Your Seatbelt" sign. Those bumps are pockets of air moving up and down. Most of the time, these bumps are in clouds. Often, planes fly above the clouds to avoid the bumps. But how high up can you go and still be in the air?

## The Atmosphere

Well, first off, when you put all the air surrounding Earth together, it's called the atmosphere. And this atmosphere extends upward from the ground for many miles until it eventually merges with outer space.

Next, we scientists like to take big things and break them down into different categories. We can break the atmosphere down into various layers, depending on whether the temperature is increasing or decreasing. The lowest layer is called the *troposphere* and the temperature decreases as you go up. It extends up to about 6½ miles. This layer is where just about all weather happens. Planes going on long trips fly near the top of the troposphere, above most of the clouds.

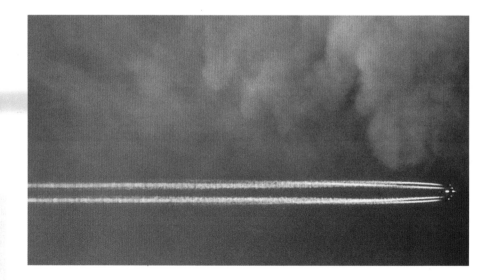

## I DIDN'T KNOW THAT!

If the world were the size of a party balloon, the troposphere would be as thick as the skin of the balloon.

# The Atmosphere All Broken Up

This illustration shows you the different layers of the atmosphere:

The top layer is the *thermosphere*, which merges with outer space. The high temperature in this layer means molecules are moving really fast, but there aren't many of them. This layer doesn't do much for our weather, but it does burn up the millions of meteoroids that hit the atmosphere every day. (You see these as shooting stars.)

Next is the *mesosphere*, where the temperature now decreases with height.

Above the *troposphere*, the temperature increases with height up to about 30 miles. We call this the *stratosphere*. The ozone layer is located here. It's responsible for filtering out most of the Sun's dangerous rays.

Not only is this bottom layer, the *troposphere*, where we live, but it's also where almost all of our weather occurs. Most of our clouds and all of our rain and snow occur in this layer.

## ASK THE EXPERT

**Q**: What's in the air we breathe?

**A**: The air contains 77 percent nitrogen, 21 percent oxygen, 1 percent water vapor (on average), .9 percent argon, and .03 percent carbon dioxide, along with dust particles, pollen, sea salt, and smoke.

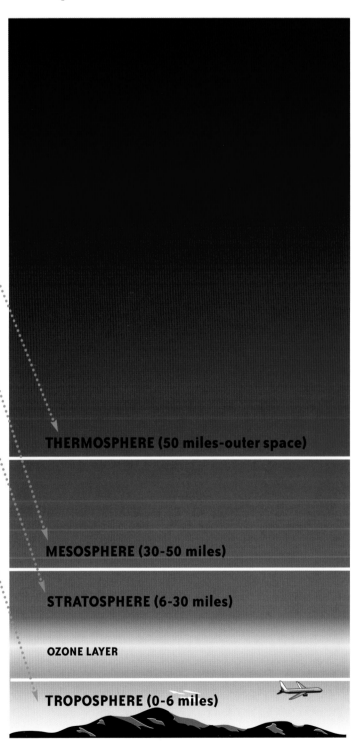

**THERMOSPHERE (50 miles-outer space)**

**MESOSPHERE (30-50 miles)**

**STRATOSPHERE (6-30 miles)**

**OZONE LAYER**

**TROPOSPHERE (0-6 miles)**

# How the Atmosphere Got Here

Where did the atmosphere come from? Well, it wasn't always here. Back in the beginning when the Earth was forming (even before I started college), there was no atmosphere and it was really hot. How hot? Let's just say that you'd need more than sunscreen to keep from literally melting. As the Earth cooled, a solid crust formed on the outside of the planet like a nice batch of homemade pudding cooling off in the fridge. The crust is the surface of the Earth where we all live. As the crust cooled, it gave off gases. This was called *degassing*. There were no oceans yet. All the water was in the air (we'll talk about water vapor later). As the Earth continued to cool, clouds formed and it started to rain. And talk about needing an umbrella. It probably rained for a few THOUSAND YEARS! That's what made the oceans. The atmosphere we have today is what was left over after the rain stopped.

## Lighter Than Air?

Now's a good time to talk about *atmospheric pressure* (or *air pressure*). Although you can't see the air, it has weight. Really! Atmospheric pressure is simply the weight of air. When you're standing on the ground, there's a lot of air above you (you're at the bottom of the atmosphere) and the pressure is greatest. You don't feel it because the pressure is distributed in all directions and there's also air inside your body pushing outward. That balances things out so you don't get squashed. Also, you're used to the air pressure where you live. Otherwise, it would feel as if there were a ton pressing against every square foot of you. Simply speaking, the more air that's on top of you, the greater the pressure. The less air that's on top of you, the lower the pressure.

**Air pressure is all around us!**

# Dr. Ed ACTIVITY

# Prove Air Has Weight

**What!? Your friends don't believe air has weight!**
**Nonsense. Show them any or all of the following activities.**

**1** Fill a glass with water to the brim. Place a piece of cardboard over it. Keep your hand on the cardboard and turn the glass upside down (do this over a sink, just in case). Take your hand away, and air pressure will hold the card in place.

**2** Get two balloons and blow one up. Tie each balloon to the end of a ruler. Try balancing the ruler on your finger. It's hard to do because the filled balloon weighs more.

**3** Let go of a helium balloon. It floats because helium is lighter than air.

**4** Put a ruler on a table with one end sticking over the edge a bit and have a doubting friend pick it up. Easy, right? Next, cover the ruler with a piece of newspaper and flatten the paper down on the table. Now try lifting the ruler. A lot harder? Why? The weight of the air is pushing down on the paper, holding the ruler down, too.

**5** If none of these work, find new friends!

# Getting All Wet for Science

One way to get a better understanding of air pressure is to look at water pressure. Pretend you're at the bottom of the ocean, with all that water pressing down on you. Air works the same way. Try this activity to see how pressure works.

## WHAT YOU NEED

Milk carton
Pen
Masking tape
Water
Deep pan

## WHAT YOU DO

**1** Empty the carton. Use the pen to poke three holes up the side of the can or carton (see illustration).

**2** Tape up the holes. Try to make them as watertight as possible.

**3** Fill up the carton with water and place it in the pan.

**4** Pull the tape off the holes, and watch how the water streams out of each of the holes. The water coming out of the bottom hole is streaming out with greatest force. There's a lot more water at top of the water on the bottom of the carton, so it squirts out with more force. The water near the top of the carton doesn't have as much water on top of it, so it sort of takes its time squirting out the hole.

# Pressure Talk

When we talk about air pressure, there are a number of different units we can use.

In the United States, air pressure is given in inches (of mercury). The normal air pressure at sea level is 29.92 inches of mercury. Weather forecasters usually use inches of mercury when talking about air pressure.

The rest of the metric world uses hecta Pascals where the normal sea level pressure is 1013.25 hPa. Millibars (mb) is another measure of air pressure commonly used by meteorologists. A millibar is the same as a hecta Pascal. Weather maps often use millibars.

You can also measure air pressure in pounds per square inch (psi). Divers, car mechanics, and engineers may use this way of measuring pressure. When you fill up your bike tire with air, and you measure how much air you put in with a tire gauge, the gauge gives you the measurement in pounds per square inch. The average sea level pressure is 14.7 pounds per square inch. That means there is 14.7 pounds per square inch pressing against you right now (if you're at sea level, anyway).

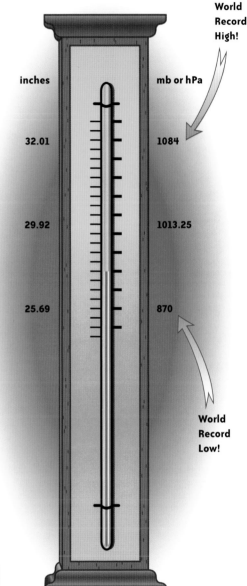

| inches | | mb or hPa |
|--------|--|-----------|
| | | World Record High! |
| 32.01 | | 1084 |
| 29.92 | | 1013.25 |
| 25.69 | | 870 |
| | | World Record Low! |

## ASK THE EXPERT

**Q: Why do we use air pressure at sea level as an average?**

**A**: Air pressure is highest at sea level because sea level is the lowest place you can go (pretty much). More air above you creates more pressure.

## I DIDN'T KNOW THAT!

**An airplane is like your bike tire. How? Well, you can't ride with a flat, can you? When you're filling up your tire with air, you're actually increasing the air pressure in that tire. If you're on an airplane flying at 35,000 feet, the air pressure up there is a lot less than what you're used to. Air is pumped into the plane to raise the pressure so you're more comfortable. The airplane's cabin becomes like your bike tire. An airplane doesn't pressurize its cabin to sea level, but to about 7,000 feet or so.**

## Dr. Ed ACTIVITY

# Altitude Affects Attitude

**Because your body is used to your current elevation and air pressure, you can notice a change when you go up or down.**

### DO THIS

If you get a chance to climb a mountain, notice what happens as you walk up. You may notice that you have to breathe harder. And although some of the hard breathing may have to do with the fact that you're walking uphill, take a rest, and notice that you still have to breathe harder up there.

### What's Happening?

As you travel up in elevation, the air gets thinner (there are less air molecules to breathe), so you have to breathe harder to get the same number of oxygen molecules you're used to.

### DO THIS

Follow your favorite home run-hitting baseball player as he travels from ballpark to ballpark. Compare how far his home runs travel in different cities. Compare the cities' elevations to see whether there's a relationship between elevation and home run distance.

### What's Happening?

A baseball hit with the same force in New York City (at sea level) will not travel as far as a ball hit in Denver, Colorado (elevation 5,000 feet). Basically, the only reason a ball stops flying after getting hit is because air pushes back against the force of the ball. The lower air pressure at higher elevations provides less resistance. So a 400-foot home run at Yankee Stadium will actually travel 425 to 430 feet at Coors Stadium in Denver.

### DO THIS

Go to a skyscraper and get on one of its elevators. As you travel upward or downward, you may notice that your ears pop. It may even hurt a little bit.

### What's Happening?

Your ears work best when the air inside them is the same pressure as the air outside. Your ears can usually adjust to a change in pressure. Sometimes, air at the old pressure can get stuck in your ears, causing some pain. By holding your nose and blowing, you're helping to get rid of the old air. You can also try drinking some water, yawning, or chewing gum.

# Measuring Pressure

**An aneroid cell barometer**

We measure atmospheric pressure with a *barometer*. Barometers come in two types. Official barometers use mercury in a glass tube. The air pressure forces the mercury up the tube. There's no air inside the tube to stop the mercury column until it reaches a balance with the actual air pressure. Normal pressure near sea level is about 30 inches of mercury.

The other, more common barometer is *aneroid*. An aneroid cell is just a small, closed container with flexible sides. The shape of the container changes with changes in pressure and can be shown on a scale that is set to inches of mercury. Aneroid barometers have an adjusting screw, which is usually in the back. This is to set the barometer to sea level pressure. All pressure readings are corrected to sea level to allow for the differences in elevation. And, yes, we can also measure pressure electronically.

## I DIDN'T KNOW THAT!

Mercury is used in a barometer (and many thermometers) because it's the heaviest liquid we have. If we used water, our barometer would have to be 30 feet tall!

## Dr. Ed, RUNNER

Once I was in Denver, Colorado, at a weather conference. A couple of friends invited me to go running with them at lunch. They were a lot older than me, so I said, "Sure!" I kept up with them for almost 100 feet before I nearly keeled over. Why? One, the elevation of Denver is 5,000 feet and the air is really thin. My friends were used to the thinner air; I wasn't. Two, my friends didn't tell me they were marathon runners.

# Make a Barometer

**You can build a barometer by making a simple version of an aneroid cell.**

## WHAT YOU NEED

Scissors

Balloon

Glass jar with a wide mouth

Rubber band

Tape

Drinking straw

Ruler

Piece of paper

Large hardcover book

Pencil

## WHAT YOU DO

**1** With the scissors, cut a piece of rubber from the balloon to stretch across the top of the jar (figure 1).

**2** Secure the rubber balloon piece around the neck of the jar with the rubber band. Make sure the covering is reasonably airtight, so the pressure inside the container won't change (at least not as quickly as the pressure outside).

**3** Tape the straw to the center of the rubber piece covering the jar (figure 2).

Figure 1

Figure 2

# High & Low Pressure Areas

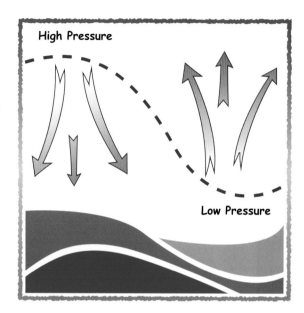

High Pressure

Low Pressure

4 Tape the ruler to the piece of paper lengthwise. Tape the paper to the cover of the book, and stand the book up. Place the jar barometer next to the book so the straw is just a hair away from the paper.

5 Check the level of the straw against the paper a few times a day and mark the locations with the pencil. Use the ruler to compare the distances between the marks. The rubber covering the jar will bulge up when the pressure outside falls, making the straw point downward. The rubber will sink down when the pressure outside is higher, because the force of the air outside is pushing down on the balloon. This makes it sink in, causing the straw to angle upward and point to a higher reading.

6 You can calibrate your barometer by checking out the local weather reports. Record the measurement of your barometer when the forecasters are saying the barometer is rising. Do the same during a storm, or when forecasters say the barometer is falling.

Sometimes your air pressure will be lower than normal, other times it will be higher than normal, and sometimes it will actually be normal. So, why isn't air pressure the same all the time? Good question. To answer this question, I need to explain what high and low pressure areas are.

High pressure areas (or highs) are like mountains of air. That means there's more air above you. So your pressure is higher.

Low pressure areas (or lows) are like valleys of air. That means there's less air above you. So your pressure is lower.

These highs and lows bring with them changes in weather. Lows are associated with clouds and precipitation, while highs are associated with clear skies.

## TRUE or FALSE

A dramatic drop in barometric pressure, not a stork, brings babies.

............................................

Midwives, obstetricians, and other professionals who deliver babies swear that a significant drop in air pressure causes very pregnant women to begin labor. But research has neither proved nor disproved this theory.

# Reaching New Heights

**If you're getting impatient with your barometer's decision not to move even one tiny fraction of an inch (hey, perhaps the weather isn't changing fast enough for you), it's time to get mobile.**

## WHAT YOU NEED

Car and responsible driver

Homemade or store-bought barometer

Paper and pencil

Bag of potato chips

## WHAT YOU DO

**1** Take a ride with your barometer. Using the paper and pencil, check and record the pressure reading before you start. Get your driver to go to the top of a steep hill or even a mountain (if you have any nearby). Check and record the pressure again. It should be a lot lower.

**2** No hills or mountains nearby? How about a tall building? Take your barometer on the elevator. You should see the same effect.

**3** Even more fun than a barometer is a bag of potato chips. Take them along as you go up the mountain or building. The outside pressure decreases, but the air pressure inside the bag stays the same, which is now more than the pressure outside. The bag will get bigger and bigger. If you're lucky, it will explode!

## Highs & Lows

**The highest pressure ever recorded at the Earth's surface was 32.01 inches (1,084 hPa) in Siberia, Russia, on December 31, 1968. The lowest pressure ever recorded at the Earth's surface was in Super Typhoon Tip in the Pacific Ocean. A reconnaissance aircraft on October 12, 1979, obtained a surface pressure of 25.69 inches (870 hPa).**

# Action in the Stratosphere: The Hole in the Ozone Layer

Ever break something? Well, we almost broke part of the atmosphere. Way above us, about 10 to 20 miles up or so, there is a layer of gas called *ozone*. Ozone is important because it absorbs a certain part of sunlight called *ultraviolet rays*, which cause us to tan (no longer such a good thing). But too much ultraviolet light causes us to burn (that's bad), and even more ultraviolet light can cause skin cancer (very bad).

Nearly 20 years ago, scientists studying the atmosphere at the South Pole discovered a hole in the ozone layer that occurred for at least part of the year. When they studied it more, they found that the ozone was being destroyed by chemicals we were putting into the air. CFCs, as they are called, were used in spray cans and in refrigeration systems. Representatives from most countries of the world got together in Montreal, Canada. They all agreed that CFCs must be phased out. Although steps have been taken to eliminate CFC production, it will take decades for the ozone layer to return to its original self. But this crisis seems to be coming to a happy ending.

**TRUE or FALSE**

When a seagull makes itself comfortable in the sand, it's going to rain.

**Possibly true,** because the density of air tends to drop prior to rain, making it harder for air current surfers, such as seagulls, to stay aloft.

# Action in the Thermosphere:
# The Northern & Southern Lights

Have you ever seen the Northern Lights (or if you're in the Southern Hemisphere, the Southern Lights)? If not, let's see if I can describe them. Sometimes, they just look like a cloud, but a cloud that glows. Sometimes, they're moving curtains of light in the night sky. They can be pale white, or brilliant red, or even green. The farther north (in the Northern Hemisphere) you are, the better your chances of seeing them. The best places to see them are Canada and Alaska. If you live in the South, your chances of seeing them are slim, but they have been seen as far south as the Gulf of Mexico.

What causes the Northern Lights (or, as they are officially called, the *Aurora Borealis*)? Ions, or electrically charged particles. There are lots of ions miles above the Earth's surface. These ions are attracted to the magnetic North Pole (the same reason a compass points north). These energetic little rascals tend to bump into each other a lot and slow down. When they slow down, they give off some of their energy. In this case, the energy is light, and that's what we see. These fantastic displays are tied to disturbances seen on the Sun and sometimes can be forecast a day or two in advance.

# Barometer Basics

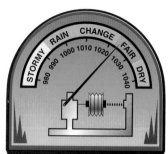

In your weather log, record the position of your barometer a couple of times a day, if you can. Or you can record changes on a day to day basis. After a few days see if you notice any relationship between the position of the barometer and the weather.

## General Guidelines

● When the pressure is falling, it usually indicates a change to bad weather. Low pressure areas normally bring clouds and rain or snow.

● When the pressure is rising, it usually indicates fair weather is in the forecast. High pressure areas bring dry air and few, if any, clouds.

● If your pressure is steady, your weather will probably not change much. This is good if your pressure is high, but not so good if your pressure is low.

## Final Note

Measuring and recording air pressure is a great measurement to start with when attempting to forecast the weather, but don't forget that temperature, wind, and humidity also play a role in weather making.

# CHAPTER 3
# Getting Warmer!

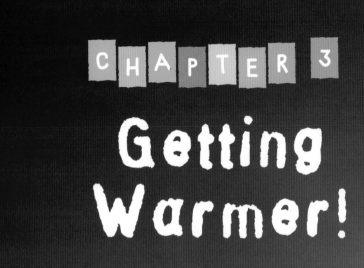

**E**VEN though the Sun is 93 million miles away from us, it's close enough to keep us warm and act as the fuel that powers our weather.

Go outside on a cool, fall day. When you stand in sunlight, you feel warm. These are the warming rays of the Sun, what we meteorologists call *solar radiation*. Radiation isn't a bad thing in this case—it's just the way the energy from the Sun gets to the Earth. In the same way the Sun warms you on that fall day, the Sun heats the Earth. And this is what helps make the weather.

# All About the Sun

Like I said on the previous page, the Sun is a star that's **only** about 93 million miles away from us. (Considering the next closest star is 24,000,000,000,000 miles away, 93,000,000 isn't so far.) Stars are balls of very hot gas. The surface temperature of the Sun (the part we see) is more than 10,000°F, but in the center of the Sun, the temperature is in the millions of degrees. The Earth receives only $\frac{1}{2,000,000,000}$ of the total amount of energy emitted by the Sun, but that seemingly small amount accounts for 99.7 percent of all the energy on Earth.

It takes Earth 24 hours to spin on its axis in respect to the Sun. This causes day and night and defines a day. It takes the Earth 365.25 days to revolve around the Sun. This defines a year. That extra quarter day is added on every four years as February 29 in a leap year.

## More Sun Facts

☼ Size: 870,000 miles across (you could fit 109 Earths across the Sun's diameter).

☼ Core temperature: 27 to 29 million degrees Fahrenheit.

☼ The Sun is a yellow dwarf star, which means it's a pretty average size as far as stars go. This term doesn't mean our Sun is tiny. There are stars that are much, much bigger, and there are stars that are much, much smaller.

☼ It takes the Sun's light 8 minutes and 20 seconds to reach the Earth.

## I DIDN'T KNOW THAT!

You could fit nearly 1.3 million Earths inside the whole Sun.

# What's Your Angle?

**Now we know that the Sun is the source of heat for us. How exactly does the Sun warm us?**

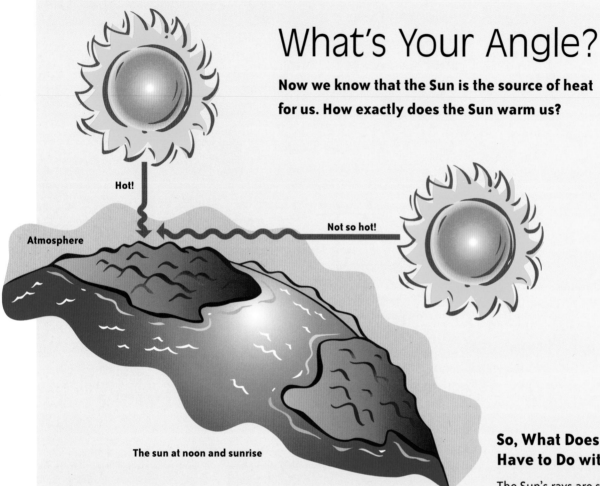

Hot!

Not so hot!

Atmosphere

The sun at noon and sunrise

## WHAT YOU NEED

Flashlight

Paper and pencil

## WHAT YOU DO

**1** Hold the flashlight (this is your Sun) directly over a piece of paper and trace around the area that is lit (it should be a circle).

**2** Next, hold the flashlight the same height above the paper but at an angle. Once again, trace the lit area.

**3** Compare the two tracings. The one with the flashlight at an angle should be bigger. The light or energy is more spread out. When the flashlight (or the Sun) is directly above, the light or energy is more concentrated and stronger.

## So, What Does This Have to Do with the Sun?

The Sun's rays are strongest around noon (the flashlight is directly over the paper), when the Sun is at its highest point in the sky. The Sun's rays are more concentrated and pass through less of the Earth's atmosphere. At sunrise and sunset, the Sun is low on the horizon (the flashlight is at an angle). The rays of the Sun are more spread out on the Earth's surface and pass through more of the atmosphere, thus weakening them.

# Hot Spots

**Here's a fun way to measure how the Sun's angle affects temperature.**

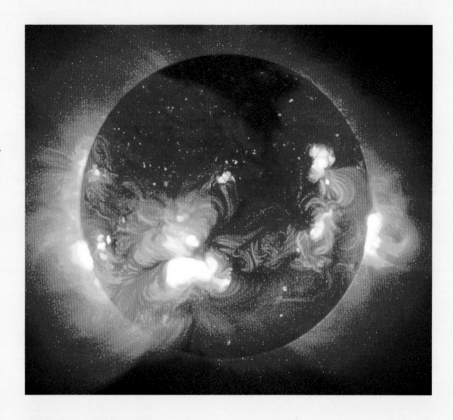

## WHAT YOU NEED

Black paint and a paintbrush

2 pieces of cardboard

Masking tape

2 thermometers

Rocks or bricks to prop up cardboard

Paper and pencil

## WHAT YOU DO

**1** Paint the two pieces of cardboard black. Once the cardboard pieces are dry, tape a thermometer to the center of each piece.

**2** Place the cardboard pieces in the shade until the thermometers read the same temperature.

**3** Place both pieces of cardboard in sunlight, one propped up by rocks or bricks until the Sun is hitting the thermometer straight on. Lay the second piece of cardboard at a lower angle.

**4** Check and record the temperatures every couple of minutes. This activity will show you how the angle of the sun influences the amount of energy or heat it creates.

# When Things Start Heating Up

You dad has asked you to mow the lawn tomorrow. The weather report is calling for a 90° scorcher. Should you mow the lawn early in the morning to get it over with, or procrastinate until 2 p.m.? Let's take a look.

The maximum heating rays from the Sun happen at noon. But it takes a while for things to heat up. The actual highest temperature usually doesn't occur until a few hours later in the afternoon. Huh? Let me explain.

When the Sun rises, you start getting its heating rays. You warm up. Incoming solar energy hits a peak around noon, when the Sun is highest in the sky. But because it takes a while for things to warm up (or, technically, to absorb this heat), the high temperature doesn't occur until a few hours later in the afternoon. The hottest temperature is late afternoon in summer, when the days are longer, and early afternoon in winter, when the days are shorter.

All this time that the Sun is sending its warming rays, the Earth's surface is sending heat back out into space. Once you get into late afternoon, more energy is leaving the surface than is coming in. You start to cool off. When the Sun goes down, you start to cool very quickly. This cooling usually continues right through the night, until you hit your low just before the Sun rises and starts heating things up again. Yes, there are things that can change this, such as cold or warm winds, but most days follow this pattern. So, my advice is to get out there and mow the lawn now!

## The Ultraviolet Index

Ultraviolet rays from the Sun tan your skin. They can also burn it or cause skin cancer. During the summer, weather forecasters will often give a number for Ultraviolet Index for the day. This number gives you an idea of how strong the Sun will be that day.

### Ultraviolet Index Chart

| UV Index | Exposure Level | Time to Burn |
| --- | --- | --- |
| 0, 1, 2 | Minimal | 60 minutes |
| 3, 4 | Low | 45 minutes |
| 5, 6 | Moderate | 30 minutes |
| 7, 8, 9 | High | 15 minutes |
| 10 + | Very High | 10 minutes |

# Talking Temperature

Temperature is how hot or cold something is when compared to something else. Of course, telling somebody how hot or cold something is could get really complicated because everybody is different. So, we have set temperature scales that everybody can relate to. The United States uses the *Fahrenheit Scale*. The rest of the world uses the *Celsius Scale*.

## Converting Fahrenheit to Celsius

**1** Subtract 32 from the Fahrenheit reading.

**2** Divide the answer by 9.

**3** Multiply that answer by 5.

*For example:*
**It's 80°F.**
80 − 32 = 48
48 ÷ 9 = 5.3
5.3 x 5 = 26.6

## Converting Celsius to Fahrenheit

**1** Multiply Celsius temperature by 9.

**2** Divide the answer by 5.

**3** Add 32.

*For example:*
**It's 18°C.**
18 x 9 = 162
162 ÷ 5 = 32.4
32.4 = 32 = 64.4

## The Thermometer

We measure temperature with a thermometer. The standard type is called a liquid-in-glass thermometer. It consists of a glass tube that's hollow in the middle. In this hollow middle, called a bore, is some liquid. As the liquid gets warmer, it expands and moves up the column. When it cools, it contracts and moves down the tube. One of the standard temperature scales, Fahrenheit or Celsius, is either etched on the glass tube or on its holder. If you're curious, the liquids used are usually mercury or alcohol with a coloring dye. Temperature can also be measured mechanically or electronically.

**Two liquid-in-glass thermometers and one electronic hermometer**

## TRUE or FALSE

Crickets can tell temperature?

•••••••••••••••••••••••••••••••••••••••••••

**Seems like they can.** Some crickets chirp faster as it gets warmer. Count a cricket's chirps for 14 seconds and add 40 to give you the temperature in Fahrenheit. Did it work?

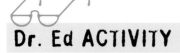

# Keep Track of the Highs & Lows

**There are two ways to keep track of the high and low temperatures for each day.**

## WHAT YOU NEED

Thermometer
Weather log
Max-min thermometer (optional)

## WHAT YOU DO

**1** Using the thermometer, measure and record the highest and lowest temperatures of the day in your weather log. Usually, the lowest temperature occurs near sunrise and the highest temperature occurs a few hours after noon.

A max-min thermometer

**2** If you have a max-min thermometer, use it to measure and record the highest and lowest temperatures each day. If you want to be official, take your reading at midnight (yes, there are people who do this). Or you can do it before you go to bed at night or when you first get up. Usually these thermometers have a digital display showing the current temperature as well as the highest and lowest figures recorded since it was reset. Simply reset it at midnight (or as close as possible) every day.

## I DIDN'T KNOW THAT!

**The range between the highest and lowest temperatures of the day in any specific place is always about the same during each particular season.**

# Hot Sand...
# Cold (Very Cold) Ocean!?

**It's the beginning of summer, and after much begging, pleading, and bribing, you convince your parents to take you to the beach. You're psyched—the sand underfoot is toasty. But wait! The water is freezing. What's up with that?**

## WHAT YOU NEED

2 pans or pie tins

Sand

Water

Ruler

2 thermometers

2 gooseneck lamps with 100-watt bulbs

Paper and pencil

Stopwatch

## WHAT YOU DO

**1** Fill one pan ½ inch deep with sand and the other ½ inch deep with water. Use the ruler to make sure they are the same depth.

**2** Place a thermometer in each tray so that the tip is under the surface of the sand or water at the center of the tray. (You may want to lean the upper part of the thermometer against the side of the pan so you can still read the temperatures.)

**3** Place a lamp about 4 inches above each tray. Each thermometer should be the same distance from the lamp. Do not turn on the lamps yet.

**4** Record the initial temperatures of the sand and the water. These values should be about the same.

**5** Turn on the lamps and let them shine on the pans. Start the stopwatch, and record the temperatures of the sand and water every 2 minutes for 30 minutes.

**6** Turn off the lamps to let the trays cool. Start the stopwatch and record the temperatures of the sand and water every 2 minutes for 30 minutes.

## What's Happening Here?

Water heats up more slowly than sand does for several reasons. The Sun's rays penetrate deeper into the water, and, because water is a fluid, it can spread the heat more evenly within itself. Water also needs more energy to raise its temperature, which means it has a higher *specific heat*, or the amount of energy required to raise the temperature of a substance by 1°C. Finally, some of the energy is used to evaporate water from the surface, so less energy is available to heat the water.

# The Reasons for the Seasons

By the way, the previous activity on page 40 not only explains why it's hotter around noon than it is early in the morning or early in the evening, but also why it's winter in the Northern Hemisphere while it's summer in the Southern Hemisphere. How? Take a look at the illustration below. As the Earth rotates, it's tilted at about a $23\frac{1}{2}°$ angle, instead of being straight up and down like a spinning top. This changes the angle at which sunlight hits the surface as Earth makes its yearly journey around the Sun. The Northern Hemisphere gets more sunlight when Earth is tipped toward the Sun, so it's hotter (summer).

At the same time, the Southern Hemisphere is tilted away from the Sun. The sunlight spreads out more thinly over a greater area there, so it's colder (winter). Also, days are longer in the summer and shorter in the winter, so when it's winter, we receive less intense sunlight and also sunlight for less time. Because the equator is in the middle of the Earth, it receives pretty much the same amount of light all year round. There is no winter there; it's summer all year long.

## Here's Another "By the Way"

Once a year, the Northern Hemisphere is tilted the maximum toward the Sun. This is when the Sun gets the highest in the sky and the rays of the Sun are best

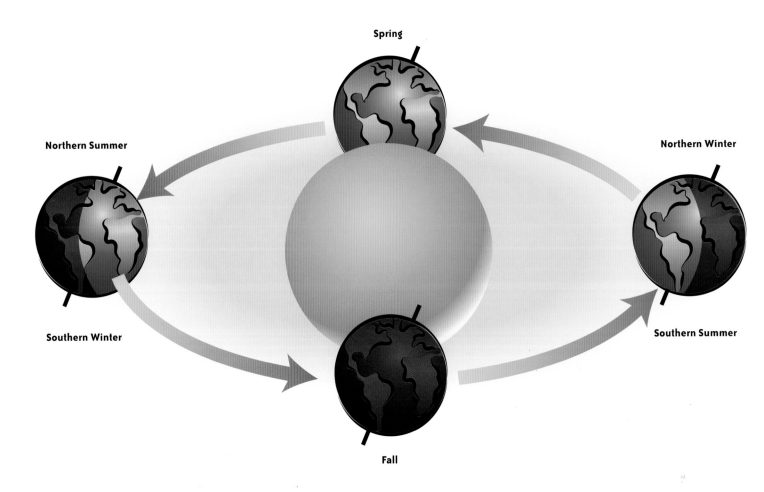

Spring

Northern Summer

Northern Winter

Southern Winter

Southern Summer

Fall

for heating. This is the *summer solstice* or the first day of summer (on or around June 21). You may say, "But doesn't it get even hotter in July and August?" Yes, once again, it takes a while for things to heat up to their maximum temperature.

Once a year, the Northern Hemisphere is tilted the maximum away from the Sun. This is when the Sun is at its lowest in the sky and the Sun's rays are weakest. This is the *winter solstice* or the first day of winter (on or around December 21). Again, the coldest temperatures often come a little later.

## Yet Another "By the Way"

An *equinox* is when day and night are exactly the same length. This happens when the Earth is not tilted in respect to the Sun. There are two equinoxes every year: the *autumnal equinox* or the first day of fall for the Northern Hemisphere (on or around September 23), and the *vernal equinox*, or the first day of spring for the Northern Hemisphere (on or around March 23). On the equinoxes, everywhere in the world has 12 hours of light and 12 hours of darkness.

## One Final "By the Way"

Many people think that summer occurs because the Earth is closest to the Sun and that the opposite is true for winter. Wrong! During its orbit around the Sun, the Earth does get closer and farther away from the Sun at times, but the differences are not important. In fact, the Earth is closest to the Sun on January 3, in the middle of our winter, and farthest away on July 3, during in our summer.

# Highs & Lows

**The highest temperature ever reported in the United States was 134°F in Death Valley, California. The lowest was -80°F in Prospect Creek, Alaska. For the whole world, the record high isn't much higher. In the Sahara Desert in Libya, it once reached 136°F. The all-time record low was an amazing -128.6°F in Vostok in the Antarctic.**

# Make a Thermometer

**Even though this thermometer would not be an effective tool for everyday use, it's cool to make something that actually tells you how the temperature is changing throughout the course of a day or week.**

## WHAT YOU NEED

Bottle with a narrow neck

Water at room temperature

Rubbing alcohol

Red food coloring

Clear drinking straw or plastic tubing

Modeling clay

White cardboard

## WHAT YOU DO

**1** Fill the bottle about one-quarter full with an equal amount of water and rubbing alcohol. Add a few drops of food coloring so you can see the mixture better.

**2** Place the straw in the center of the bottle opening and seal the hole of the bottle with clay, keeping the straw in the middle. Make sure the straw doesn't touch the bottom of the bottle and the clay makes a tight fit.

**3** Place the white cardboard behind the straw so you can mark changes in the level of the water. Heat and cool the bottle (get an adult to help you heat the bottle), and note changes in the level of water in the straw. The water level should go up when you heat it and down when you cool it. Even simply putting this device in your hands will affect the temperature reading.

# Three Thermometer Activities

**Here are some experiments you can do with a thermometer or two.**

### Measure Temperature Differences at Different Heights

Outdoors, place one thermometer right on the ground (but out of sunlight during the day.) Put another up as high as you can get it (in the shade) and read it safely. During the day, the one on the ground should read higher because temperature usually decreases with height. The same should hold true at night when there's a good breeze. But on clear, calm nights, the temperature near the ground is often colder. This is called an *inversion*. By the way, if you do this indoors, the opposite would happen, because heat rises. The air near the ceiling would be warmer.

### Measure the Temperature in Different Places

Does your family car have a thermometer in it? If so, you can see how the temperature changes from place to place. If you have any big hills or mountains nearby, try driving to the top. During the day or at night when there's some wind, you should see the temperature drop as you go up. On a clear, calm morning around sunrise, try driving down into a valley. On these mornings, it often gets colder as you go down. This is called *cold air drainage*, and this simply means that cold air will sink to the lowest point if there is no wind to mix the air. If you live near a city, try driving around on a clear, calm night. It should be warmer where you have a lot of buildings. This is called the *urban heat island*, and this happens because concrete and asphalt absorb the heat of the day and keep it warmer at night. Open areas such as parks are usually colder.

### Measure the Temperature in the Sun and Shade

Put two thermometers outside. Put one in full sunlight and one in the shade. Write down the difference in temperature between the two thermometers. Which do you think is the official temperature? The one in the shade is the official temperature—the temperature of the air. The thermometer in the sunlight is measuring the heating effect of the Sun's rays.

# The Greenhouse Effect

If you don't have a greenhouse, roll up the windows of your car on a sunny day. It gets hot inside. The glass windows let the sunlight in, and that heats everything inside the car. But the windows don't allow cooler air to mix in from the outside. The atmosphere is sort of like this. It lets in the sunlight that heats the Earth's surface but it absorbs the heat energy being emitted from the surface. Here's another way to look at this: Some of the Sun's energy is trapped and recycled by the atmosphere. Overall, this is a good thing, because without an atmosphere the Earth would be a lot colder (like below freezing!).

One of the gases that traps the Earth's heat is carbon dioxide. Although carbon dioxide has always been in the atmosphere, there is more now than there was 100 years ago. We put carbon dioxide into the atmosphere whenever we burn fossil fuels (oil, coal, and gas), and when we clear and burn rain forests.

The Earth has also been getting warmer over the past hundred years. Have we caused this warming by increasing the amount of carbon dioxide in the atmosphere? Many scientists think so, and they have urged governments around the world to take steps to reduce carbon dioxide emissions.

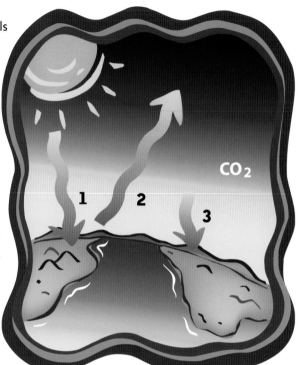

**1. Absorbed radiation**
**2. Reflected radiation**
**3. Trapped radiation**

# Why We Don't Freeze to Death Every Night

**Sure, the Sun keeps us warm during the day, but did you know that our atmosphere keeps us from freezing at night? This activity shows you how.**

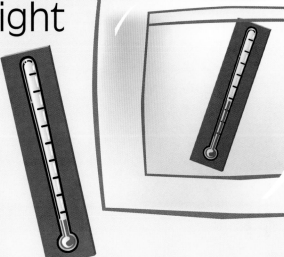

## WHAT YOU NEED

2 thermometers

Sandwich-size plastic bag

Quart-size plastic bag

2 twist ties

## Highs & Lows

The Indian Ocean is the warmest: its surface water temperatures is typically over 70°F year-round. The Arctic Ocean is the coldest ocean: its surface water temperature typically hovers around 32°F.

## WHAT YOU DO

**1** Place one thermometer into the sandwich bag. Inflate the bag, and tie it up with a twist tie to keep the air from escaping.

**2** Place this bag into the quart-size bag. Inflate the bigger bag and tie it as well.

**3** Place this strange-looking device in sunlight. Place the second thermometer in the same location. Leave the thermometers for 15 to 30 minutes.

**4** Check out the temperature readings on both thermometers. The one in the bags should show a higher temperature than the one next to it.

**5** Now put the thermometers in a cool, dark place. After 15 to 30 minutes, check out the two temperature readings again. The thermometer in the bag should still have a higher temperature.

## What's Happening Here?

Think of the air inside the two bags as our atmosphere, and the thermometer inside is the Earth. The plastic bags (our atmosphere) trap some of the heat from the Sun and keep us a lot more comfortable at night. If Earth were like the unbagged thermometer, we'd freeze to death every night.

## I DIDN'T KNOW THAT!

Rhododendrons can tell temperature, too. The leaves are fully open when it's warm, but they start to close with colder temperatures. The leaves will fully close when the temperature gets down to 20°F.

# Neat Things You Can See in the Sky

## Rainbow

A rainbow is an arc of color from violet to red produced on a curtain of falling rain droplets; the raindrops act as prisms to break up the sunlight into the various colors. Always look directly away from the Sun to see a rainbow. The Sun has to be fairly low in the sky, so look to the west in the morning or east in the evening. Sometimes there can be a second bow outside the first, with the colors reversed.

## Sundogs

Bright spots on either or both sides of the Sun are called sundogs. These are caused by cirrus clouds.

**TRUE or FALSE**

Another word for a sundog is starpooch.

**False:** But don't let that stop you from creating your own weather lingo. (The synonym for sundog is *weathergaw*.)

## Halos

These are bright rings around the Sun or Moon caused by high, cirrus clouds.

## Crepuscular rays

These are rays of the Sun made visible by clouds.

# What Causes Wind

Wind is caused mostly by pressure differences that are, in turn, caused by temperatures differences. Take a sea breeze, for example. This is an onshore wind at the coast that usually develops during the warmest part of the day. This is how a sea breeze is created:

**1** The land heats up a lot faster than the water (see page 45).

**2** This causes the hot air just over the land to rise, like water in a fountain. The pressure above increases. Now, stay with me here.

**3** This air above needs some place to go, so it travels toward lower pressure areas up there, which in this case, happens to be above the water. This creates an upper-level wind that blows from warm to cold (land to water). This

also causes the pressure on the land surface to decrease.

**4** Now, as this air gathers over the water, the pressure at the surface of the water rises. The air right over the water will move toward land (toward the new low created by this process), and there's your sea breeze. At night, the opposite happens.

Sea breeze

Land breeze

## I DIDN'T KNOW THAT!

**Wind direction is always the direction from which the wind is blowing and is given as a compass point (north, northeast, north-northeast, etc.). So, a north wind is coming from the north.**

# Measuring the Wind

There are two components of the wind that we measure: direction and speed. Wind direction is usually found by using a wind vane, which, in its simplest form, is just some type of an arrow that can spin around with the wind. The head of the arrow will point in the direction from which the wind is coming.

Wind speed is usually measured with an anemometer, which has three or four cups mounted on it to spin with the wind.

Both instruments can be connected either mechanically or electronically to display the wind direction and speed. If you don't have an anemometer handy, you can estimate wind speed using the Beaufort Scale (see page 59). This

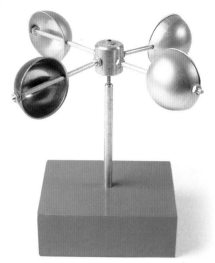

**An anemometer**

relates wind speed to things you can see. Wind speed is given in miles per hour in the U.S., in knots (nautical miles per hour—1 knot = 1.15 mph) for aviation and marine purposes, and in either meters per second or kilometers per hour in the metric system.

## 👉 Highs & Lows 👈

Port Martin, Antarctica, made the record books for both the highest mean wind speed in a day (108 mph, based on wind measurements taken each hour) and the highest mean wind speed for a month (85 mph, based on wind measurements taken each day). If it weren't so near the site of the world's lowest temperature (see page 47), it might be a good place to go windsurfing.

**A wind vane**

# Create a Wind Vane

**If you just want to build a simple wind vane by yourself, try this one out. You'll need to bring it inside when you're done.**

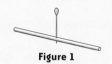

**Figure 1**

**Figure 2**

## WHAT YOU NEED

Sharpened pencil with new eraser

Template (see page 127)

Card stock or posterboard

Scissors

Straw

Straight pin

Glue or tape

Modeling clay

Small plastic food container with lid

Enough pebbles to fill the container halfway

Permanent marker

Compass

## WHAT YOU DO

**1** With the pencil, trace the template figures on page 127 onto the posterboard, and cut out the shapes.

**2** Cut the straw so it's 5 inches long.

**3** Stick the straight pin through the center of the straw (figure 1).

**4** Snip a ½-inch slit in each end of the straw (figure 2). Place the arrow pointer and tail into the slits in the straw. Use a dab of glue to keep them in place.

**5** Place a mound of clay on the inside center or the container's lid. Fill the container half way or so with the pebbles. (This will keep the wind vane from getting blown away.)

**6** Place the lid on the container and turn the container upside down.

**Figure 3**

**7** Poke a hole in the bottom center of the container wide enough for the pencil. Place the pencil through the hole in the bottom of the container and make sure you wiggle it past the rocks so that it sticks into the clay (figure 3).

**8** Stick the pin into the pencil's eraser.

**9** With the permanent marker, write "N," "S," "W," and "E" for the four principal directions on the container.

**1 0** Take the wind vane outside and place it in a location without a lot of obstacles (up high is a plus). Use the compass to find north, and position your wind vane in the correct direction. You may have to widen the holes in the straw so that it moves easily around the pin. Do this by carefully wiggling the straw.

# The Beaufort Scale

The Beaufort scale has been used to estimate wind speeds for nearly 200 years. Admiral Sir Francis Beaufort of the British Navy created this scale in 1806 to help estimate wind speed by describing what the wind did to war ships. Over the years, this scale has been changed to include descriptions of land effects.

The Beaufort scale is divided into a series of values, from 0 for calm winds to 12 for hurricanes. See the next page for more.

0-1

2-3

4-5

6-7

8-9

10-12

# THE BEAUFORT SCALE

| FORCE (15 feet above ground) | EQUIVALENT SPEED (mph/knots) | DESCRIPTION | SPECIFICATIONS |
|---|---|---|---|
| 0 | 0–1 / 0–1 | Calm | Smoke rises vertically |
| 1 | 1–3 / 1–3 | Light air | Direction of wind shown by smoke drift but not by wind vanes |
| 2 | 4–7 / 4–6 | Light breeze | Wind felt on face; leaves rustle; ordinary vanes moved by wind |
| 3 | 8–12 / 7–10 | Gentle breeze | Leaves and small twigs in constant motion; wind extends light flag |
| 4 | 13–18 / 11–16 | Moderate breeze | Dust and loose paper moved by wind; small branches moved by wind |
| 5 | 19–24 / 17–21 | Fresh breeze | Small trees in leaf begin to sway; crested wavelets form on inland waters |
| 6 | 25–31 / 22–27 | Strong breeze | Large branches in motion; umbrellas used with difficulty |
| 7 | 32–38 / 28–33 | Near gale | Whole trees in motion; difficulty walking against the wind |
| 8 | 39–46 / 34–40 | Gale | Twigs break off trees; wind makes it hard to walk |
| 9 | 47–54 / 41–47 | Severe gale | Slight structural damage occurs (chimney pots and roof tiles removed) |
| 10 | 55–63 / 48–55 | Storm | Seldom experienced inland; trees uprooted; considerable structural damage occurs |
| 11 | 64–72 / 56–63 | Violent storm | Very rarely experienced; accompanied by widespread damage |
| 12 | 75+ / 64+ | Hurricane | Structural damage on land and storm waves at sea |

# Wind-Worthy Vane

**If you can get an adult to help you, this wind vane is a lot stronger and can stay outside.**

## WHAT YOU NEED

Small saw

Piece of scrap wood,
  1 x 2 x 12 inches

Hammer

Nail

Marker

Template (see page 127)

Aluminum sheeting
  or old pie plate

Scissors or tin snips

Glue

Metal washer

Old broomstick
  or dowel

Wire

## WHAT YOU DO

**1** Use the small saw to cut a ½-inch-deep vertical slit at each end of the 12-inch-long piece of wood.

**2** Hammer a nail all the way through the top center of the piece of wood.

**3** Take the nail out and hammer it in again at the bottom of the piece of wood. Keep alternating hammering the nail in at the top and bottom until the piece of wood spins easily around the nail.

**4** With the marker, trace the template onto the aluminum sheeting. Use the scissors to cut the arrow pieces out of the aluminum sheeting.

**5** Glue the arrow pieces into the slits you made in step 1. Let the glue dry.

**6** Place the washer on the nail, and hammer the nail in the piece of wood into the old broomstick or dowel (see illustration). Don't hammer the nail all the way in. Make sure the wind vane moves freely.

**7** You can mount your wind vane on a fence post with the wire. Try to get the vane as high above the ground as possible, but make sure it's secure.

## I DIDN'T KNOW THAT!

**The first known wind vane was in the form of a brass statue of the god Poseidon located in Athens, Greece. It dates back to the year 50 B.C.**

60

# Watch the Wind

**Farmers used wind vanes to figure out when the wind changed directions. This information let them know whether cold air was coming, a storm was on its way, or conditions would be just right for their crops. Simply paying attention to the direction of the wind can get you attuned to the weather coming your way.**

## WHAT YOU NEED

Wind vane

Compass

Weather log and pencil

## WHAT YOU DO

**1** For the period of a week, use your wind vane and compass to pay attention to what direction the wind is coming from. Write down the direction in your weather log. Check it out as many times a day as you can.

**2** Notice when the wind changes directions and also what changes (if any) occur in the weather. See whether you can figure out any relationship between wind direction and overall weather.

**Tree uprooted by strong winds**

# Wind Chill Factor

Not only can you feel the wind, but the wind also makes you feel colder. The wind can actually blow heat away from your body. The wind chill factor adds together the actual temperature and the cooling effect of the wind. Using the table below, you can see that when it's 20°F and the wind is blowing at 20 mph, it actually feels like it's 4°F.

## TEMPERATURE (°F)

| Calm | 40 | 35 | 30 | 25 | 20 | 15 | 10 | 5 | 0 | -5 | -10 | -15 | -20 | -25 | -30 | -35 | -40 | -45 |
|------|----|----|----|----|----|----|----|----|----|----|-----|-----|-----|-----|-----|-----|-----|-----|
| 5 | 36 | 31 | 25 | 19 | 13 | 7 | 1 | -5 | -11 | -16 | -22 | -28 | -34 | -40 | -46 | -52 | -57 | -63 |
| 10 | 34 | 27 | 21 | 15 | 9 | 3 | -4 | -10 | -16 | -22 | -28 | -35 | -41 | -47 | -53 | -59 | -66 | -72 |
| 15 | 32 | 25 | 19 | 13 | 6 | 0 | -7 | -13 | -19 | -26 | -32 | -39 | -45 | -51 | -58 | -64 | -71 | -77 |
| 20 | 30 | 24 | 17 | 11 | 4 | -2 | -9 | -15 | -22 | -29 | -35 | -42 | -48 | -55 | -61 | -68 | -74 | -81 |
| 25 | 29 | 23 | 16 | 9 | 3 | -4 | -11 | -17 | -24 | -31 | -37 | -44 | -51 | -58 | -64 | -71 | -78 | -84 |
| 30 | 28 | 22 | 15 | 8 | 1 | -5 | -12 | -19 | -26 | -33 | -39 | -46 | -53 | -60 | -67 | -73 | -80 | -87 |
| 35 | 28 | 21 | 14 | 7 | 0 | -7 | -14 | -21 | -27 | -34 | -14 | -48 | -55 | -62 | -69 | -76 | -82 | -89 |
| 40 | 27 | 20 | 13 | 6 | -1 | -8 | -15 | -22 | -29 | -36 | -43 | -50 | -57 | -64 | -71 | -78 | -84 | -91 |
| 45 | 26 | 19 | 12 | 5 | -2 | -9 | -16 | -23 | -30 | -37 | -44 | -51 | -58 | -65 | -72 | -79 | -86 | -93 |
| 50 | 26 | 19 | 12 | 4 | -3 | 10 | -17 | -24 | -31 | -38 | -45 | -52 | -60 | -67 | -74 | -81 | -88 | -95 |
| 55 | 25 | 18 | 11 | 4 | -3 | -11 | -18 | -25 | -32 | -39 | -46 | -54 | -61 | -68 | -75 | -82 | -89 | -97 |
| 60 | 25 | 17 | 10 | 3 | -4 | -11 | -19 | -26 | -33 | -40 | -48 | -55 | -62 | -69 | -76 | -84 | -91 | -98 |

(Left axis label: WIND (mph))

## Dr. Ed, SKIER

The year I lived in northern Vermont, I took up skiing (there was nothing else to do, and I lived on the side of a mountain). On New Year's morning, I walked outside and it felt okay. Although the thermometer read -15°F, it was calm and sunny. Good skiing weather, I thought. (Hey, what did I know?) I walked over to the ski slope, slapped on my skis, and took off downhill. I almost died. Dummy! When you're moving, you generate your own wind chill effect. Two minutes on the slopes and an hour in the lodge and I was ready to get back home. The chairlift wasn't much better, and then I still had to ski back to my place. My glasses iced up (not steam, ice). My beard was filled with ice from my breath. And I had frostbite on my fingertips, despite wearing huge gloves.

# The Chilling Truth

**Here's a simple way to show that wind chill factor and temperature are not the same thing.**

## Highs & Lows

The strongest wind ever recorded at the Earth's surface was on Mt. Washington in New Hampshire, USA. On April 12, 1934 the anemometer read 231 mph! Meteorologists think that winds in the strongest tornadoes may get even higher than that, perhaps approaching 300 mph.

## WHAT YOU NEED

2 thermometers
Windy day

## WHAT YOU DO

**1** Place both thermometers outside in the shade. Make sure one is in the wind and the other is sheltered from it (behind a board or in a large box).

**2** After 15 minutes, check the readings. They should be the same, no matter how cold that wind is making you feel. Wind chill is felt only by people and animals, and it doesn't affect the actual temperature reading.

# Make an Anemometer

**Here's a simple device that will show you whether or not the wind is strong. Again, this one you can build by yourself, but it's not as durable as the one on page 65.**

## WHAT YOU NEED

4 drinking straws

Tape

Stapler

4 small paper cups

Straight pin

Sharp pencil with unused eraser

Marker

## WHAT YOU DO

**1** Form a cross out of the four straws and tape them at the center (figure 1).

**2** Staple the top side of one of the cups to one end of the straw cross (figure 2).

**3** Repeat with the other three cups, making sure all the cups face the same direction.

**4** Push the pin through the center of the cross. Then push the pin into the eraser of the pencil (figure 3). Make sure the straw contraption moves easily by blowing on it.

**5** Color one of the cups with the marker so you can identify it when counting how many times the anemometer turns.

**Figure 1**

**Figure 2**

**Figure 3**

# Wind-Worthy Anemometer

**If that helpful adult is still around, you can build this sturdier anemometer.**

## WHAT YOU NEED

Piece of wood, $\frac{3}{4}$ inch x 3 feet

Piece of plywood, $\frac{3}{4}$ x 5 x 5 inches

Hammer

2 nails, 1 inch long or longer

Wood glue

$\frac{5}{8}$-inch metal washer

2 pieces of wood trim, $\frac{1}{4}$ x 1 x 36 inches

Vegetable oil

Acrylic craft paint and paintbrush

4 yogurt cups or other plastic cups

4 tacks

## WHAT YOU DO

**1** Stand the $\frac{3}{4}$ inch x 3-foot post on one end, and center the piece of plywood on top of it. Have an adult help you hammer one of the nails through the center of the plywood into the end of the piece of wood. This is the stand for the anemometer. Flip it over so it stands.

**2** Glue the washer, centered, on top of the post.

**3** Make a cross out of the two pieces of wood trim, and glue them together.

**4** Once the glue has dried, hammer the cross into the post, making sure the nail goes through the hole in the washer you glued into place in step 2. Leave $\frac{1}{2}$ inch of the nail exposed above the post so the crosspiece will spin.

**5** Give the cross a whirl to see whether it spins smoothly. You can rub vegetable oil on the washer to reduce friction between the parts.

**6** Paint the outside of one of the plastic containers and let it dry.

**7** Tack the bottom or side of each container to the ends of the crosspieces. Also use glue to reinforce the cups. Make sure the ends of the cups all face the same direction.

# Take Your Anemometer for a Walk

**Wind can be affected by where you live. Not sure what I'm talking about? Well, then, take a walk.**

## WHAT YOU NEED

Homemade or
  store-bought anemometer

Stopwatch

Paper and pencil

## WHAT YOU DO

**1** Find different locations to place your anemometer. Try behind your mom's minivan, in the backyard, in front of your house, between your house and your neighbor's house, and wherever else you think wind speed might vary.

**2** In each location, use the stopwatch to count how many times the anemometer spins in one minute. Make notes with the paper and pencil.

## ASK THE EXPERT

## What's Going On?

Depending on where you live, local conditions can produce variations on wind. We've already discussed the sea breeze on page 55, which is one example. The same thing can happen along large lakes in summer. If you spend much time in a city, you've probably noticed places where the wind blows a lot stronger. Wind can be channeled between large buildings and concentrated along narrow streets.

The same effect occurs in the mountains. Another local wind found in the mountains is the down slope breeze at night. Cold air sinks down the sides of the mountains on relatively calm nights, producing a noticeable breeze. Up slope flows can occur during the heat of the day.

**Q**: Can you figure out exactly how fast the wind is traveling with a homemade anemometer?

**A**: With some effort, you could count the number of revolutions your anemometer makes in a minute to figure out how fast the wind is; however, if the wind is blowing strongly, you won't be able to count fast enough! Use the Beaufort Scale to determine wind speed when filling out your weather log.

# Coriolis:
## Another Factor that Causes Wind

When you start talking about winds on a bigger scale, you have to allow for factors other than just air pressure. One biggie is Coriolis. I'll try not to get too technical here. Simply put, the Earth spins. The spin of the Earth makes the wind curve and spin, too. Also, in the Northern Hemisphere, Coriolis causes highs to spin clockwise and lows to spin counterclockwise. What about the Southern Hemisphere? Highs and lows go in the opposite direction.

**How winds would move if Earth didn't spin**

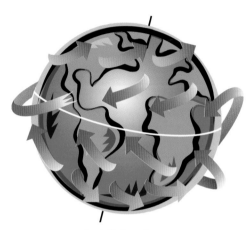

**Coriolis in action**

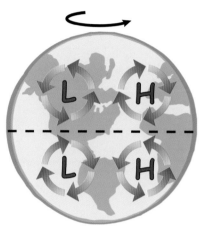

**Wind direction of lows and highs**

# Large-Scale Wind Systems

Besides the normal highs and lows you see on the daily weather maps, there are other highs and lows which basically stay put all the time and generate large-scale wind systems.

Near the equator (where it's always hot) we find a belt of low pressure at the surface, pretty much produced the same way the low over the ground was in our sea breeze example. The high pressure areas in this case are found in the subtropics (as far south as Florida). Air will try to flow from the highs to the low but be curved to the right by Coriolis. The results are northeasterly to easterly winds known as the Trade Winds. In the Southern Hemisphere, the curving is to the left, and southeasterly winds result but are still called the Trade Winds.

In midlatitudes (most of the United States, northern hemisphere; southern Australia in the southern hemisphere), the winds try to blow toward the Poles in both hemispheres, but again are curved by Coriolis. In both cases, the result is westerly winds simply known as the Westerlies. You most likely live in the Westerlies, and most of your weather systems move from west to east.

## I DIDN'T KNOW THAT!
The term "Trade Winds" comes from the old sailing days. These reliable winds were great for the ships traveling from Europe to the New World.

**Westerlies**

**Trade winds**

# Jet Streams: It's Breezy Up Here

Have you ever noticed that in a river the current is usually much stronger in the middle than along the banks? The atmosphere is the same way. The winds usually get much stronger as you go up. Normally, they hit their peak about five miles up. This is called the *jet stream*, a sort of river (or stream) of air in the atmosphere. Winds can be very strong in the jet stream—sometimes 200 to 300 mph. Usually, they blow from west to east, but they can also come from the north or south.

Sometimes, there are two different jet streams—one to the north and one to the south. The northern one usually separates cold air in the north from warmer air in the south. When this jet stream dips down to the south, cold air will come with it. If it stays to the north, the weather will stay warm. The southern jet stream doesn't affect temperature as much. But it can bring storms and heavy rain and occasionally even heavy snow. Seldom are both jet streams strong at the same time. Usually, one or the other is stronger and more dominant, often for the entire winter.

During the summer, the northern jet stream weakens and retreats to the north, normally along the U.S./Canada border. The southern jet stream disappears altogether.

Although these jet streams are very high up, they have an important effect on our weather. In the Northern Hemisphere, the jet stream has a massive effect on the formation of high and low pressure zones, and thus greatly influences our weather.

High clouds affected by the jet stream

# El Niño and La Niña

El Niño is one of the most famous weather events. What is it? At times, the Trade Winds weaken and the ocean waters of the tropical South Pacific, rather than being blown westward with the winds, sit in the tropical sunshine and become unusually warm. A lot of heat goes up into the atmosphere there, especially in winter. To move this excess energy, the winds pick up aloft. The southern branch of the jet stream becomes very strong. This effect is most noticeable in winter. The southern jet stream energizes storms along a southern storm track. California is usually the first place to be hit by these storms. High winds, flooding rains, and heavy mountain snows occur there. The storms continue eastward, bringing rains to the South and Southeast. Sometimes, these storms turn up along the East Coast and become major storms. The northern states tend to be dry during El Niño winters. They're also usually very warm

Ask the EXPERT

**Q**: What is wind shear?

**A**: Wind shear is a sudden change in wind speed or direction. This is especially hazardous to airplanes. Numerous major plane crashes have been caused by wind shear. Most airports are now equipped with instruments that can detect sudden changes in the wind.

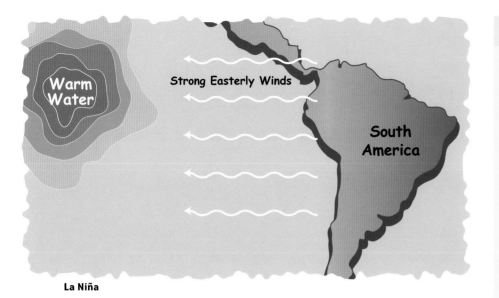

**La Niña**

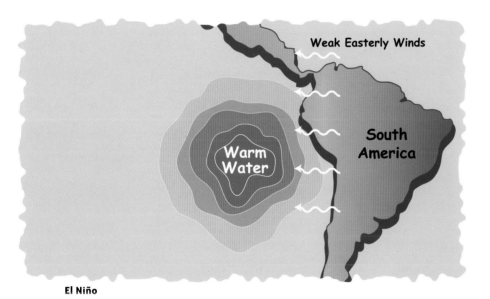

**El Niño**

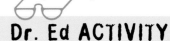

# Track El Niño & La Niña

**What were winters like in your area for the following years? Did they fit the El Niño/La Niña pattern?**

**1997–98:** strong El Niño

**1998–99:** strong La Niña

**1999–00:** strong La Niña

**2000–01:** weak La Niña

**2001–02:** neither

**2002–03:** weak El Niño

**2003-2004:** neither

because the southern jet stream keeps most of the cold air locked up north in Canada. The main effect El Niño has in summer and fall is fewer hurricanes forming in the Atlantic. The same strong winds aloft that fuel winter storms help keep tropical storms from forming.

La Niña is the opposite of El Niño. The Trade Winds strengthen, more water is transported quickly across the Pacific, and ocean temperatures in the tropical South Pacific are unusually cold. The southern jet stream is much weaker. There are few southern storms in winter. Most of the storms stay north, coming ashore in the Pacific Northwest and moving along the northern tier of states. In this case, the North is wet and the South is dry. Very often it's also warm throughout the U.S. because the strong northern jet stream bottles up the cold air in Canada. During hurricane season, the weaker winds in the South usually mean more and stronger storms in the Atlantic.

How do we ever have cold winters in the U.S. if both the El Niño and La Niña bring warm weather? If neither is going on or if they are weak, other factors can bring cold air to the lower 48 states.

**69**

# What Winds Bring with Them

You can start adding reports on wind direction and speed to your Weather Log. If you don't have a wind vane, you can just go outside and feel which direction the wind is blowing from. You can also use the Beaufort scale to estimate wind speeds.

Wind moves the air from place to place and often brings with it the weather of the place it is coming from. For example, north winds bring in colder air from the north, and south winds bring warmer air from the south. (Of course, if you lived in the Southern Hemisphere, you reverse this because it's cold to the south and warm in the north.) When the air has been over water for a long time, an onshore wind will often bring clouds and precipitation. Take this into consideration when forecasting the weather.

In particular, note the wind direction at your location and the type of weather you have. Over time, you should be able to come up with a forecasting scheme that relates wind direction to expected weather. During the winter, keep the wind chill in mind.

**WEATHER ADVISORY: HIGH WINDS = RUINED UMBRELLAS!**

# CHAPTER 5

**Y**OU can't see it, but on some days you'll definitely feel it. Yes, there's water in the air, and water is the last ingredient in the weather recipe.

When water is a solid or liquid, you can see it in the air in the form of clouds, rain, and snow. But when water is a gas, you can't see it. But it's there. How do I know? Last summer, my basement flooded because the air conditioner wasn't working right. Where did all that water come from? The air! Besides cooling the air, air conditioners take moisture out of it. When we talk about humidity we're referring to the water or water vapor that's in the air.

# The Wet Stuff That Isn't Rain

# Water Vapor & Relative Humidity

Water in the form of a gas is called *water vapor*, and *humidity* is how much water vapor is in the air. You may ask where the water vapor in the air came from. Most of it comes from the oceans. When liquid water changes to a gas, we say it *evaporates*. When your favorite TV weather people talk about humidity, they almost always talk about the *relative humidity*. This has nothing to do with their relatives. It's the amount of water vapor in the air at the moment compared to how much the air could hold at *saturation*. When the air is saturated, it can't hold any more water vapor and the relative humidity is 100 percent. Saturated air doesn't mean it has to be raining out.

So, we have a nice percentage to tell us how much water vapor is in the air. Good, huh? No! The problem is that the amount of water vapor the air can hold changes with the temperature. In other words, warm air can hold more water vapor than cold air can. For example, if you raise the temperature of air by 20°F, the air can hold twice as much water vapor. This means that the relative humidity can change even though the amount of water vapor in the air stays the same. This happens all the time. When you wake up in the morning and it's cool and foggy, the relative humidity is 100 percent. By afternoon, it's warm and the relative humidity may be down to 30 percent. But, there's been no change in the actual amount of water vapor in the air.

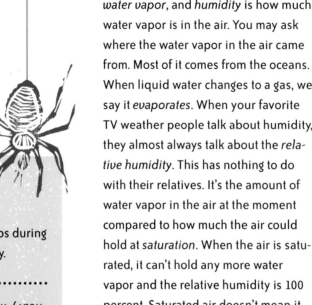

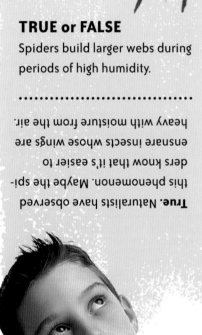

Some major fog

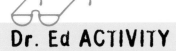

## Dr. Ed ACTIVITY

# Evaporate It!

**Try this activity at different times of the year, and during different weather conditions to see how evaporation is affected.**

### WHAT YOU NEED

Any container with straight sides
  and a flat bottom

Water

Ruler

### WHAT YOU DO

**1** Fill the container with water. Place the container outside, preferably in sunlight.

**2** Measure how much water is in it.

**3** Measure the water level again the next day. The amount the water level has gone down is the amount of evaporation you have had. On a hot day in summer, especially if the air is dry, ¼ to ⅓ of an inch of water can evaporate.

**An official evaporation pan**

# It's Not the Heat, It's the Humidity

Have you ever heard that saying before? Perhaps one summer afternoon when you complained about how hot you were? Well, the saying has some truth to it.

You feel hotter when the air is warm and moist rather than when it's hot and dry. Why? The body cools itself by evaporating sweat. Dogs cool themselves by panting and evaporating saliva (you may want to try this). When the air is dry, more sweat evaporates and you don't feel as hot. When it's humid, sweat can't evaporate as fast and your body gets hotter.

So, if your body responds to both heat and humidity, then you'll feel cooler if the temperature is lowered or if the amount of water vapor in the air is reduced. That's what an air conditioner does (when it's working right).

## I DIDN'T KNOW THAT!

Moist air is lighter than dry air. Most people think the opposite is true. I could prove this scientifically, but I don't want to bore you.

## Dr. Ed, TENNIS PLAYER

Once I played tennis in Denver, Colorado. It was over 90°F, but I didn't feel hot at all because the air was so dry. (Of course, I wound up drinking gallons of liquids, which is what you should do to prevent dehydration.) Another time, I played in Middletown, Connecticut. It was 75°F but very humid. I almost croaked.

# Check Out the Humidity

**Okay, you've just learned a bunch about humidity.
Now go outside and check it out for yourself.**

## WHAT YOU NEED

Local weather report

Pencil and paper

## WHAT YOU DO

**1** A few times a day, find the humidity in your local weather report. Note the humidity and time.

**2** Notice what effect the humidity is having on you as you play, do chores, or simply hang out outside. Write down whether or not you feel comfortable, hot, cold, etc. What happens to your sweat? How's your breathing?

**3** After doing this for a week or so, you may be able to predict what it will feel like outside simply by checking out the relative humidity.

## I DIDN'T KNOW THAT!

If you've had trouble opening or closing a drawer or door that worked fine the day before, it could be due to a change in humidity. Wood absorbs moisture, causing it to swell and expand.

# Measuring Humidity

There are a number of instruments we use to measure humidity. A *psychrometer* has two thermometers, one with a cloth wick around it. By wetting the wick and letting the water evaporate, the cooling effect is noted on that thermometer. Using prepared tables and comparing that temperature with the actual temperature shown on the other thermometer, you can determine relative humidity. A *hair hygrometer* uses human hair as a sensing element. You bad-hair-day people out there know that hair changes with humidity. It actually changes length. This effect can be used to show relative humidity. Humidity can also be measured electronically.

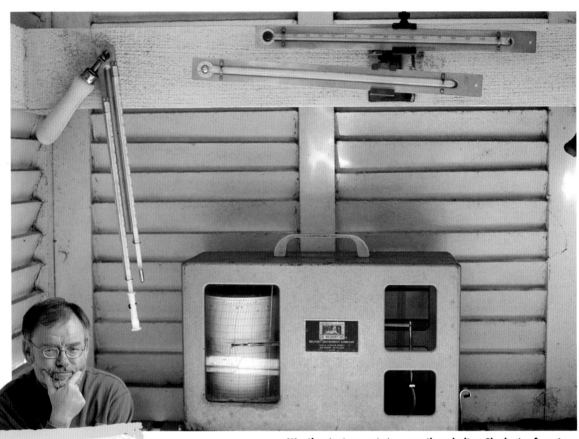

Weather instruments in a weather shelter. Clockwise from top left: psychrometer, a max-min thermometer, and a hygrothermograph, which measures both temperature and humidity.

**ASK THE EXPERT**

**Q: Does humidity affect any of our five senses?**

**A:** Yes, in a way. We don't actually become more sensitive, but humidity intensifies sounds and sights so that we see and hear more clearly. How? Sound waves and light rays travel better in high humidity.

# Dewpoint

Is there anything else we can use that better describes the amount of water vapor in the air? Well, we could use the *dewpoint*, which is the temperature you need to cool down air to cause saturation to occur. When fog forms in the morning, the air has been cooled to its dewpoint. Dewpoint is a measure of humidity, but it's given as a temperature. Clouds and fog form when the air is cooled to the dewpoint. People can sense dewpoint, too, especially in summer.

## Dr. Ed ACTIVITY

# Measure the Dewpoint

**Here's a simple way to figure out the dewpoint of a glass of ice water.**

### WHAT YOU NEED
Glass
Water
Thermometer
Ice

### WHAT YOU DO

**1** Fill a glass with water at room temperature. Put the thermometer in the glass.

**2** Add some pieces of ice and stir.

**3** The temperature of the water will go down. Keep doing this, and watch the outside of the glass. As soon as the glass begins to "steam up" with little water droplets, check the temperature of the water. Congratulations! You've reached the dewpoint.

# The Heat Index

This is sort of like the opposite of wind chill. The *heat index* is a combination of temperature and humidity and is given as a temperature value you feel under certain conditions. On the chart below, find your current temperature and relative humidity, and follow down and across until you find where the values meet. Read off the temperature. This is the heat index, or how hot it actually feels outside.

## HEAT INDEX TABLE

| Relative Humidity (%) | Air Temperature (°F) | | | | | | | | | | |
|---|---|---|---|---|---|---|---|---|---|---|---|
| | 70 | 75 | 80 | 85 | 90 | 95 | 100 | 105 | 110 | 115 | 120 |
| 30 | 67 | 73 | 78 | 84 | 90 | 96 | 104 | 113 | 123 | 135 | 148 |
| 35 | 67 | 73 | 79 | 85 | 91 | 98 | 107 | 118 | 130 | 143 | |
| 40 | 68 | 74 | 79 | 86 | 93 | 101 | 110 | 123 | 137 | 151 | |
| 45 | 68 | 74 | 80 | 87 | 95 | 104 | 115 | 129 | 143 | | |
| 50 | 69 | 75 | 81 | 88 | 96 | 107 | 120 | 135 | 150 | | |
| 55 | 69 | 75 | 81 | 89 | 98 | 110 | 126 | 142 | | | |
| 60 | 70 | 76 | 82 | 90 | 100 | 114 | 132 | 149 | | | |
| 65 | 70 | 76 | 83 | 91 | 102 | 119 | 138 | | | | |
| 70 | 70 | 77 | 85 | 93 | 106 | 124 | 144 | | | | |
| 75 | 70 | 77 | 86 | 95 | 109 | 130 | | | | | |
| 80 | 71 | 78 | 86 | 97 | 113 | 136 | | | | | |
| 85 | 71 | 78 | 87 | 99 | 117 | | | | | | |
| 90 | 71 | 79 | 88 | 102 | 122 | | | | | | |
| 95 | 71 | 79 | 89 | 105 | | | | | | | |
| 100 | 72 | 80 | 91 | 108 | | | | | | | |

| Heat Index | How It Affects the Human Body |
|---|---|
| 130° or above | heat stroke likely with continued exposure |
| 105° to 130° | heat stroke likely with prolonged exposure |
| 90° to 105° | heat stroke possible with prolonged exposure |

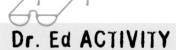
# Build a Psychrometer

**This contraption will give you a pretty accurate reading of the current relative humidity.**

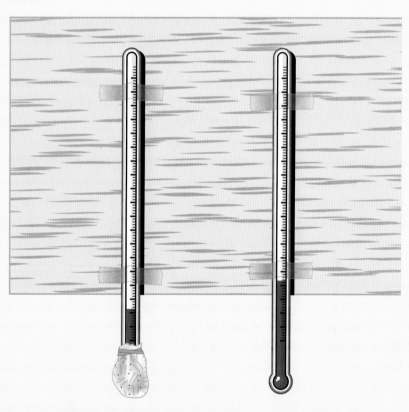

## WHAT YOU NEED

Piece of cardboard

2 liquid-in-glass thermometers

Tape

Small piece of cotton cloth or gauze

Small rubber band

Pencil and paper

## WHAT YOU DO

**1** Fold the piece of cardboard so that it can stand by itself.

**2** Carefully tape the thermometers side by side on the board with the bulbs hanging down below the board.

**3** Wrap the small piece of cotton around the bottom of one of the thermometers, and use the rubber band to keep it in place. Hey, you've got a psychrometer.

**4** To take a reading, wet the piece of cotton (the wick) and blow on it. Write down the temperatures on both thermometers. The temperature on the plain thermometer is called the dry bulb temperature. The temperature on the thermometer with the cloth wick is called the *wet bulb temperature*. With these two values and the table on page 125, you can calculate the relative humidity.

## Highs & Lows

**On any given day of the year, it's pretty hot in Dellol, Ethiopia. Dellol has the world's highest annual mean temperature—94°. When you factor in the heat index, the mean temperature jumps to over 100°.**

# Build a Hair Hygrometer

**This instrument works under what's commonly known (at least to me) as the bad-hair-day principle. High humidity increases hair length, while low humidity causes it to shrink. Hair hygrometers have been used to measure humidity since the 1700s. Here's a fun one you can build.**

## WHAT YOU NEED

Straight hair at least 8 inches long
Shampoo and water
Towel
Shoebox
Tape
Straw
Glue
Modeling clay
Marker
Hairdryer

## WHAT YOU DO

**1** "Borrow" several strands of hair from someone with long hair. You want the strands to be at least 8 inches long. It also helps if you can find thick hair. Really thin hair is hard to work with.

**TRUE or FALSE**

Scientists have been measuring humidity with hair hygrometers for at least 500 years.

**2** Wash the hair with a drop or two of shampoo, and rinse it well with water to get rid of any dirt or oil. Dry the hair with a towel before using it.

**3** Stand the shoebox on its long side and tape one end of the straw to this side (figure 1).

**4** Tie a piece of hair close to the taped end of the straw. Use a drop of glue to make sure the hair stays in place.

**5** Attach the other end of the hair to the top of the box. Make sure the hair is now holding up the straw (figure 2). Adjust it if the straw is lying on the bottom of the hygrometer.

**6** Place a small amount of clay on the free end of the straw to act as a weight (figure 3). Make sure the hair is taut.

**7** To calibrate the hygrometer, place it in the bathroom the next time you take a hot shower. Close all windows and doors so you can make sure the relative humidity in the room will be 100 percent.

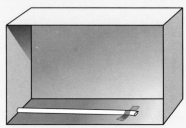

**Figure 1**

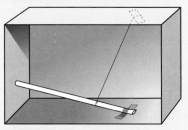

**Figure 2**

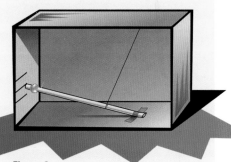

**Figure 3**

**8** Mark where the straw is pointing, and label it "100%." To find 0 percent, place the hygrometer in a dry place and blow it with the hairdryer. Use the no-heat setting. That should get you close to 0 percent. Mark where the straw is pointing and label it "0%." Now your hygrometer is ready (figure 3).

True.

# Hazy, Hot & Humid

Humidity is one of the most important factors in determining our weather. In the next chapter, I'll talk about how clouds and precipitation are formed. This is all the result of water vapor in the air. So, measuring humidity is crucial in making good forecasts. And, as we have also noted, it's important to how we feel.

## General Forecasting Guidelines

Increases in humidity usually mean an increase in cloudiness and a chance of precipitation. Decreases in humidity mean fewer clouds and fair weather coming in.

It's time to start adding humidity measurements to your weather log. Depending on what instrument you made or information you can get from other weather sources, start recording the relative humidity and/or dewpoint every day. Note whether the humidity has been increasing or decreasing.

WEATHER WATCH: HUMIDITY RISING? WEATHER COULD TAKE A TURN FOR THE WORSE.

# Water, Water Everywhere

# CHAPTER 6

**W**HEN water is in the air, it's no big deal. But when it starts falling to the ground, then you've got some weather to write home about.

In the last chapter, we talked about relative humidity and how it's affected by temperature. If the air cools, it can't hold as much water vapor. The relative humidity goes up. Remember dewpoint? It's the temperature at which saturation occurs. So, if the air continues to cool, at some point the temperature will equal the dewpoint, the relative humidity will be 100 percent, and the air will become saturated. Then an interesting thing happens—some of that water vapor changes back into water droplets (it *condenses*) or ice crystals (it *crystalizes*), depending on whether the temperature is above or below freezing. Yes, you've got rain or snow.

# Dew & Frost:
# Water Vapor's Reappearing Act

If water condenses on the ground, we call it dew. This is why the grass is often wet in the mornings. It didn't rain overnight. The moisture came right out of the air and condensed on the grassy surface. If the temperature is below freezing, you'd get frost. Frost happens when the water vapor crystallizes into those white ice crystals common in the cold season. It never was liquid water; frost isn't frozen dew. The best conditions for forming dew and frost are clear skies and no wind. Clear skies allow the heat of the day to escape into the atmosphere during the night. A lack of wind means warmer air doesn't mix down from above.

**TRUE or FALSE**
Dew in the morning means no rain.

••••••••••••••••••••••••••••••••••

**This is usually true** because the best conditions for dew formation are clear skies.

Do we have dew? Yes we do.

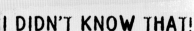

# I DIDN'T KNOW THAT!

Plants can be killed by cold even without a visible frost occurring. What damages plants is water freezing inside the plant, not the frost on the outside of plants. Orange trees have been known to explode during extreme cold.

# Fog:
# Nature's Way to Slow Traffic

Suppose a whole layer of air near the ground is cooled to saturation? Then you get condensation in the entire layer—what we call fog. Fog is basically a cloud that's in contact with the Earth's surface. There are different types of fog.

● Radiation or ground fog is very common in the early mornings. Like dew and frost, it develops best under clear skies and calm winds. It is more common in valleys and usually burns off later in the morning.

● Frontal fog comes with a front (we'll talk more about fronts in Chapter 8). Often coming ahead of a warm front, frontal fog is widespread and can last for many hours.

● Marine fog develops over marines. Just kidding. It develops over cold water.

## I DIDN'T KNOW THAT!

**Many people think that steam coming off boiling water is water vapor. Wrong. You can't see water vapor. If you see steam, the water vapor has already condensed.**

# Clouds

Air cools at night, but it also cools when it's lifted. This is what produces clouds.

## So, what causes lifting?

● Air rises when it's heated strongly by the Sun. In the summer, we often see big, billowy clouds form.

● Low pressure areas have rising air in the middle. Lows almost always have clouds with them.

● When wind blows up the side of a mountain, it's lifted. Clouds often form over mountains.

● And, finally, air rises over cold and warm fronts, forming clouds.

## ASK THE EXPERT

**Q: How much do clouds weigh?**

**A:** Clouds weigh millions of pounds. They don't come crashing to Earth because the rising air that makes the clouds keeps them up.

## What are Clouds Made Of?

Clouds are made of tiny water droplets or ice crystals, depending on whether the temperature is above or below freezing. The cloud particles are so small that they remain suspended in the air. That's why clouds don't fall to the ground. Clouds can occur near the Earth's surface and up to 10 miles above it. Scientists love to classify things, so we classified clouds. We break them down into low, middle, and high clouds, depending on how high up they are. See the next four pages for more on clouds.

## I DIDN'T KNOW THAT!

Fog and clouds have a hard time forming if the air is too clean. Water vapor likes to condense on small impurities in the air. We call these impurities *condensation nuclei*.

### TRUE or FALSE

A halo around the Sun or Moon means it will rain or snow soon.

. . . . . . . . . . . . . . . . . . . . . . . . . . .

**This is not always right,** but halos indicate increasing moisture above, which often precedes a storm.

# Cloud Chart

There are clouds that extend through several layers—the clouds of vertical development: nimbostratus, cumulus, cumulus congestus or towering cumulus, and cumulonimbus

**High clouds (above 20,000 feet):** cirrus, cirrostratus, and cirrocumulus

**Middle clouds (between 6,500 and 20,000 feet):** altocumulus and altostratus

**Low clouds (below 6500 feet):** stratus, stratocumulus, and fractostratus or fractocumulus

# More on Clouds

## High Clouds

Okay, while you look at the pretty pictures, I'll describe what each cloud is. Let's start with the high clouds.

***Cirrus*** looks like cotton candy being pulled. It has whitish wisps of cloud and usually indicates fair weather.

***Cirrostratus*** is a whitish sheet completely covering the sky. You can see right through it. It's cirrostratus that produces halos around the Sun or Moon. Although rain or snow doesn't come from cirrostratus, it often precedes precipitation by a day or two.

***Cirrocumulus*** is a patch or sheet of little white puffy clouds. It usually indicates fair weather.

## Middle Clouds

***Altocumulus*** is also a patch or sheet or puffy clouds, but these are lower than cirrocumulus and the clouds themselves are bigger and may be white or gray. No rain or snow makes it to the ground from these clouds, and they can precede fair weather or bad, depending on the situation.

***Altostratus*** is a grayish or whitish sheet completely covering the sky. It doesn't produce halos, and the Sun can be seen vaguely through it. Altostratus indicates increasing moisture in the atmosphere and usually precedes precipitation by 24 hours or less.

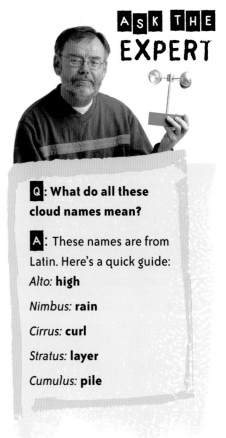

## ASK THE EXPERT

**Q**: What do all these cloud names mean?

**A**: These names are from Latin. Here's a quick guide:

*Alto:* **high**

*Nimbus:* **rain**

*Cirrus:* **curl**

*Stratus:* **layer**

*Cumulus:* **pile**

## Low Clouds

**Stratus** is a low, dull, grayish sheet completely covering the sky and totally obscuring the Sun during the day. By itself, it can produce only drizzle or very light rain or snow. If there are deeper clouds above, the rain or snow can be heavier.

**Stratocumulus** is a sheet of big puffy white or gray clouds that are often in dark patches or rolls. Showers of rain or snow are possible and can be heavy.

**Fractostratus** and **fractocumulus** are ragged pieces of cloud usually beneath the main cloud deck. They are often dark and fast moving and often accompany bad weather. They're sometimes called scud.

## Clouds of Vertical Development

**Nimbostratus** is a dark gray layer of large, puffy clouds whose bottoms are often hidden by falling rain or snow, which may be heavy. These are your winter storm clouds.

**Cumulus** are large, individual puffy clouds that look like white cauliflower on top. The bottoms are often dark and flat. This type of cumulus cloud brings good weather.

**Towering cumulus** are very tall clouds whose tops are still puffy and white but whose bottoms are very dark. They can produce showers and may develop into thunderstorms.

## Other Cloud Types

**Mammatocumulus** are dark, rounded protrusions often hanging below the anvil of a thunderstorm cloud. When they are large and very prominent, they often precede severe thunderstorms.

**Lenticular clouds** are shaped by the wind and are rounded or lens shaped. They are common in mountainous areas. They warn pilots of turbulence caused by air blowing over the mountains.

**Cumulonimbus** are the thunderstorm clouds. They extend way up into the atmosphere and have flattened tops called *anvils*. They are very dark at the bottom and can produce very heavy rain and lightning.

**Virga** are cloud streaks below the base of a cloud. They are caused by rain or snow falling from a cloud.

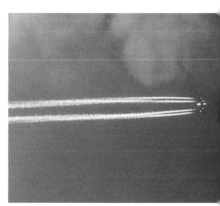

**Contrails** are those long, narrow white clouds you often see behind jet airplanes. The moisture comes out of the engines and condenses in the very cold air high above.

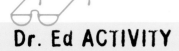
# Make Your Very Own Cloud

**The simplest way to make a cloud is to go outside on a cold day and exhale. The water vapor coming out of your mouth will immediately condense. You "see your breath." That's a cloud. Want something a little more elaborate? Try this.**

## WHAT YOU NEED

Cork to fit bottle opening

Small nail

Plastic tubing

Warm water

Plastic 2-liter soda bottle

Ball pump

Wooden match (optional)

## WHAT YOU DO

**1** Make a hole through the cork with the nail so your plastic tubing fits very snugly. Place one end of the tubing in the hole.

**2** Put some warm water in the bottle. Put the cork in the mouth of the bottle.

**3** Connect the other end of the tube to the pump.

**4** Pump air into the bottle. At some point, the cork will pop off due to the air pressure inside the bottle. When that happens, the pressure inside the bottle will decrease rapidly. This causes a quick cooling of the air to its dewpoint and a cloud should form.

**5** For a better cloud, put some condensation nuclei (see page 86) in the air in the bottle before you seal it. How? Have an adult light a wooden match, blow it out, and drop it into the bottle. (The smoke particles from the extinguished match will attract condensing water vapor.)

# WEATHER CHALLENGE:
## THE ULTIMATE
# Cloud Quiz

**For this quiz, simply match up the cloud with its name and also with the forecast usually associated with that cloud.**

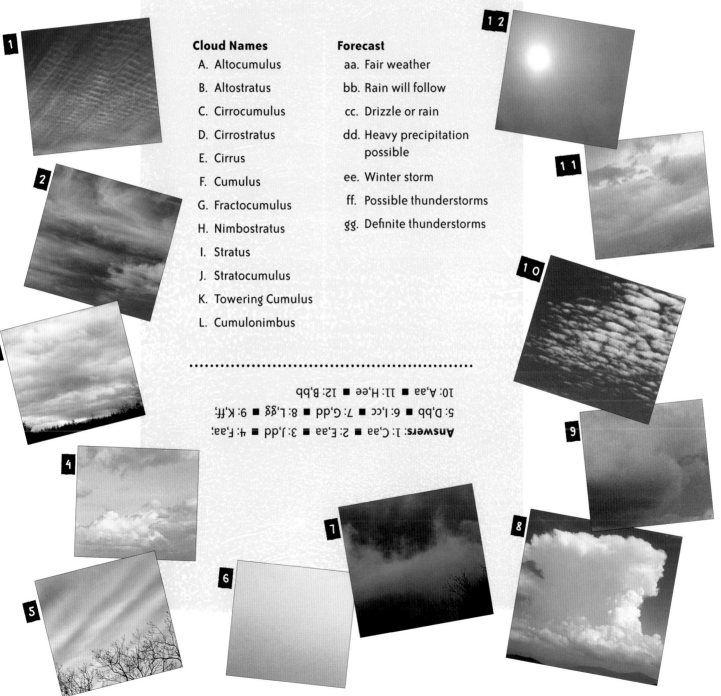

### Cloud Names
A. Altocumulus
B. Altostratus
C. Cirrocumulus
D. Cirrostratus
E. Cirrus
F. Cumulus
G. Fractocumulus
H. Nimbostratus
I. Stratus
J. Stratocumulus
K. Towering Cumulus
L. Cumulonimbus

### Forecast
aa. Fair weather
bb. Rain will follow
cc. Drizzle or rain
dd. Heavy precipitation possible
ee. Winter storm
ff. Possible thunderstorms
gg. Definite thunderstorms

**Answers: 1:** C,aa ■ **2:** E,aa ■ **3:** J,dd ■ **4:** F,aa; **5:** D,bb ■ **6:** I,cc ■ **7:** G,dd ■ **8:** L,gg ■ **9:** K,ff; **10:** A,aa ■ **11:** H,ee ■ **12:** B,bb

# Check Out the Clouds

**Got your head in the clouds? Good. Keep observing, and see whether you can notice how clouds are good indicators of future weather.**

## WHAT YOU NEED

Cloud photos on pages 87 through 89

Weather log

## WHAT YOU DO

**1** Go outside and, using the cloud pictures, see what type or types of clouds are out there. You can keep a daily weather log of this or add it to your daily weather observation.

**2** Pay careful attention to the clouds when you travel. Different places often have different types of clouds.

**3** Record what happens during the day weatherwise as you watch the clouds.

**ASK THE EXPERT**

**Q**: Can clouds produce frozen rain in the summer?

**A**: You bet! Strong thunderstorms extend so high up that the top part of the cloud has temperatures well below freezing. Pieces of ice can form there and grow until gravity makes them fall to the ground. This is what we call *hail*. Most hail is small—pea to marble size. But during very strong thunderstorms, hailstones can grow to the size of baseballs or even softballs!

# Precipitation? Precisely.

Precipitation is either liquid or frozen water that falls from a cloud. Remember, clouds are made of tiny water droplets or small ice crystals that stay suspended in the air because they're so small. If they become too big, the rising air currents that produced the cloud can't hold them up any more and they fall to Earth. Either the ice crystal grows into a snowflake or a water droplet becomes a raindrop.

So why do some clouds produce rain or snow and others don't? Often it depends on how much moisture is in the air and how strongly the air is lifted. More moisture and stronger lifting usually mean precipitation. The causes of lifting (and in this case, precipitation) are the same as we discussed for cloud formation, but the lifting is stronger.

## Different Types of Precipitation

What can I say about rain? It's wet. That's because it's liquid water with a temperature above freezing. If the rain droplets are very small, we call it drizzle. Smaller yet and we've got mist. Boring as it may sound, rain is the most common type of precipitation in most areas.

But if temperatures get below freezing, then we get some good stuff. Every weather fanatic loves snow. Why? Maybe because it's weather made visible. It's also weather with an impact. Snow consists of ice crystals. They form in clouds where the temperature is below freezing. These ice crystals have six sides and an infinite variety of patterns.

**A**<sub>sk</sub> **T**<sub>he</sub>
## EXPERT

**Q: Why is snow white?**

**A**: Although ice is colorless, the crystal structure of a snowflake bends and reflects light waves, so we see white.

# Gauge the Rain

**Precipitation is measured with a rain gauge, which is simply a water-tight container that collects the precipitation and usually makes reading the amount easy.**

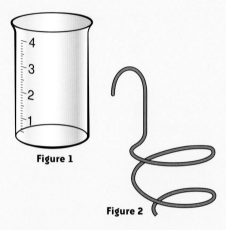

Figure 1

Figure 2

## WHAT YOU NEED

Clear glass beaker

Masking tape

Ruler

Permanent marker

Coat hanger or wire

## WHAT YOU DO

**1** When choosing a container to use for your rain gauge, make sure it has straight sides. That is, the top must have the same diameter as the bottom, or you'll throw off your readings (figure 1).

**2** Place a strip of tape vertically along the outside of the gauge. Use the ruler and marker to mark off ⅛-inch measurements on the tape.

**3** Devise a contraption to hold your rain gauge with the coat hanger or wire. Use figure 2 to help you if you want. Make sure you create a hook so you can hang up your gauge.

# Now, Measure Precipitation

**See whether your measurements are the same as those of your weather forecaster.**

## WHAT YOU NEED

Rain gauge

Weather log

## WHAT YOU DO

**1** Put the rain gauge outside in an open spot. Make sure there is nothing overhead, such as trees, wires, or a roof, because these can direct rainwater into or away from your gauge. For example, hang your gauge on the edge of a fence or some other structure that's not too close to any houses or buildings.

**2** Wait for rain, take daily measurements, and keep records in your weather log. Don't forget to empty your gauge every day.

# Sleet & Freezing Rain

Wintertime can also bring two other types of precipitation.

Sleet is actually frozen rain. These small ice pellets form when rain falls through a below-freezing layer of air near the surface and freezes while still in the air.

Freezing rain or glaze occurs under similar conditions. But in this case, temperatures are only below freezing in a very shallow layer near the ground. The rain doesn't freeze until it makes contact with the surface and then it covers everything with ice. Freezing rain makes traveling very dangerous and does tremendous damage when trees and power lines break under the weight of the ice.

**Freezing rain**

**Heavy icing often damages trees.**

## I DIDN'T KNOW THAT!

It can snow with surface temperatures above freezing. As long as it's below freezing aloft and the above freezing layer near the ground is shallow, it can start snowing with temperatures in the 30s, 40s, and rarely even 50s.

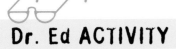

# Stovetop Water Cycle

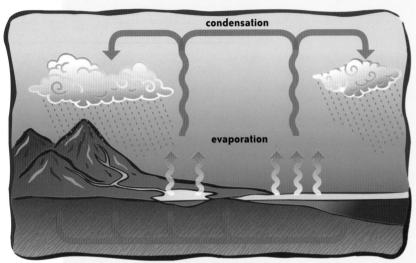

condensation

evaporation

**The water cycle in action**

If you've been following along, you know that water evaporates (becomes gas), condenses (becomes liquid or solid again), falls to Earth as precipitation, and then evaporates again, starting the whole process over. Yes, nature recycles. We call this the *water cycle*. With an adult helper, you can recreate the water cycle on a smaller scale in your kitchen.

## WHAT YOU NEED

2 pans
Water
Stove

## WHAT YOU DO

**1** About an hour or so before doing this activity, place one of the empty pans in the refrigerator.

**2** An hour after doing step 1, fill the second pan with water and heat it on the stove until it's boiling.

**3** Take the cold pan out of the fridge, and hold it a few feet above the boiling water. (Don't get too close to the steam because it will burn you.)

**4** In the boiling pan, the liquid water is turning to water vapor. In the cold pan, the vapor is condensing back into liquid water and, if your aim is good, the water should fall back into the hot pan. Dude, you're a water cycler.

# The All-Wet Roundup

Now we have more things to add to our daily weather log. Note whether you have dew, frost, or fog in the morning. Keep track of which type of clouds you have. You can do this just at a certain observation time or keep records throughout the day. Often there is more than one type of cloud in the sky at one time. This just means there is moisture at different levels of the atmosphere. Note whether you have any precipitation and, using your rain gauge, record how much. During the winter, record the type of precipitation you get. Use your ruler to measure accumulations of snow and sleet. Melt the frozen precipitation to get a liquid water equivalent.

For forecasting, keep in mind that dew, frost, and fog usually develop under clear skies. You can use the cloud information I gave you to make a forecast based on cloud type.

97

# CHAPTER 7

# Weather with an Attitude

EVERY Weather Fanatic I know is fascinated by some type of severe weather, be it tornadoes, thunderstorms, hurricanes, or all three. It's not that we want to see people get hurt. It's just the pure force of the weather that we love.

Severe weather is weather that can damage property (buildings, fences, bridges, etc.), injure people, or (at its worst) take lives. Some people ignore the weather most of the time. You can't ignore severe weather: it's noisy when it happens and everybody talks about it for days before and after it. Strangely enough, in the overall scheme of things, severe weather isn't that important. More often than not, weather goes about its business of moving heat and water around without any major problems for us.

Only a few storms get strong enough to be severe weather. Even then, they're no problem as long as they don't hit anything. Keep in mind, weather only becomes a hazard if we're in the way!

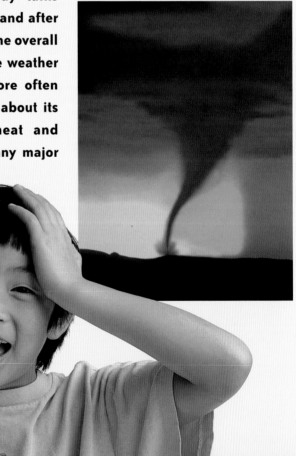

# Thunderstorms: Bright Lights, Big Noise

Although they can occur at any time of year, thunderstorms are most common in the summer. Cumulus clouds, feeding off warm and moist air, grow quickly during the day, driven by heat from the Sun. These clouds can be more than 10 miles high. (Good thing there's lots of room in the atmosphere.) The rising air in the core of the cloud, the *updraft*, can move at almost 100 mph. These clouds cause a lot of interesting things. Rainfall rates can be excessive; you can pick up an inch of rain in 15 minutes. But, of course, what makes a thunderstorm is lightning.

## Lightning

Lightning is an electrical discharge in the atmosphere. Ever touch something and get a shock? Sometimes you'll even see a spark of light. That's *static electricity*. Lightning is like that but a whole lot more. As cumulus clouds grow tall, they develop an electrical field. The top of the cloud, where there are many ice crystals, is usually positive. The bottom part of the cloud, which is filled with rain droplets, is usually negative. The ground under the cloud is relatively positive. An electrical charge builds up and the atmosphere has to relieve itself (so to speak).

That's when a lightning bolt occurs. It can be within a single cloud, between two clouds, or from the cloud to the ground. Most lightning bolts that hit the ground come from the bottom of the cloud. Occasionally, a bolt comes from the top of the cloud—a *positive giant*.

**An anvil cloud forming**

## Thunder

*Thunder* is simply the sound made when a lightning bolt heats the air and the air expands quickly. Because sound moves much slower than light, you can judge how far away a lightning bolt is by counting the seconds between seeing the flash and hearing the thunder. Each 5 second interval equals 1 mile. And don't be afraid of thunder: it's the lightning that's dangerous.

**Electric charges**

**Electric charges moving toward each other**

**An electrical discharge—lightning!**

# The Dangers of Thunderstorms

How dangerous is lightning? Each year in the United States alone, about 60 people are killed by lightning and another 200 are injured—many are left with permanent disabilities. Where is it safe to be during a thunderstorm? Inside a building or in a car. By the way, it's the metal frame of the car, not the rubber tires, that protects you. The worst place to be is in an open field such as a ball field. Don't go under trees—lightning seeks the tallest object. Being in, near, or on the water can be very dangerous. And, yes, people can be killed while on the phone during a thunderstorm—even a cordless phone. The "30/30 Rule" is now recommended for lightning safety. If the thunder following a lightning bolt is heard within 30 seconds, take shelter. And stay inside until 30 minutes after the last rumble of thunder is heard.

## I DIDN'T KNOW THAT!

Although a lightning bolt seems to come down from a cloud, electrical charges also go up from the ground to meet it. If you feel your hair standing on end during a thunderstorm, that's what's happening. Take cover immediately or drop to the ground before you get hit by lightning!

## TRUE or FALSE

Benjamin Franklin's kite was struck by lightning when he flew it in a thunderstorm.

**False:** The kite wasn't hit by lightning. The sparks he saw were due to the highly charged atmosphere during the storm. If the kite had been hit by lightning, old Ben would have been fried. Others who tried this experiment wound up that way.

# Thunderstorm Facts

● Lightning detection networks can show where lightning strikes are occurring. Displays are often shown on TV weather shows.

● Florida gets more thunderstorms than any other state in the U.S. Some places get hit by more than 100 storms a year. The island of Java in Indonesia has thunderstorms more than 300 days a year!

● Heat lightning at night is caused by a distant thunderstorm. The sound of the thunder dies out before it reaches you.

● *Ball lightning* is a continuous electrical discharge in the form of a glowing ball.

● The fear of lightning is called *astraphobia*. (It's also called common sense.)

● The fear of thunder is called *brontophobia*.

● There are more than 100,000 thunderstorms in the United States each year and 16 million storms around the world. At any moment, it's estimated that there are 2,000 thunderstorms going on, producing 100 lightning strikes per second.

● A line of thunderstorms is called a *squall line*. If the middle of a squall line begins to stick out, it's called a *bow echo*, and it will probably produce damaging winds.

## ASK THE EXPERT

**Q: Who keeps an eye out for thunderstorms?**

**A:** The Storm Prediction Center (SPC) in Norman, Oklahoma, is the government agency in charge of thunderstorm forecasting. Check out their website (http://www.spc.noaa.gov/) for the latest forecasts and storm reports. The SPC issues thunderstorm watches for areas where severe thunderstorms may develop. If a severe thunderstorm is actually occurring, a warning will be sent out by the local National Weather Service (NWS) Office for the county or counties affected. This means take cover!

# Lightning in a Jar

**Ever walked across a carpet in your socks, reached for a doorknob, and—zzzhht—gotten a shock? Lightning works the same way. Make lightning in a bottle to see for yourself.**

## WHAT YOU NEED

Aluminum foil

Scissors

Ruler

Copper wire

Modeling clay

Glass or plastic drink bottle

Comb

Carpet

## I DIDN'T KNOW THAT!

**This activity generates about 100 volts of electricity. Real lightning generates more than one million volts.**

## WHAT YOU DO

**1** Cut a ¼ x 2-inch wide piece of foil. Set it aside for a moment.

**2** Push the wire through a piece of modeling clay that's big enough to cover the opening in the bottle. You want the wire to hang down into the bottle.

**3** Bend one end of the wire into a hook. Hang the piece of foil on the hook.

**4** Put the hook and foil in the bottle, and seal the bottle with the modeling clay.

**5** Rub the comb on the carpet. Touch the wire with the comb. If the comb is charged, the foil strip will stand apart from the wire. Now the foil is charged.

**6** To discharge the foil of its electricity—and get a jolt—touch the wire.

# Severe Thunderstorms

Although all thunderstorms are dangerous (because they produce lightning), some strong storms are classified as severe and special warnings are sent out for them. A severe storm produces strong winds, large hail, or tornadoes. Only about 10 percent of all thunderstorms are classified as severe. The strongest of the thunderstorms are called *supercells*. These are the storms most likely to be severe.

## Other Hazards

Besides lightning, there are other hazards associated with thunderstorms. Large hail can damage property and especially crops. Hailstorms do hundreds of millions of dollars of damage in the United States each year.

*Flash floods* are rapidly developing floods in streams and small rivers. They often accompany slow-moving thunderstorms. Dozens of people die each year in these floods—many of them drive their cars right into the fast moving-waters and are swept away. Some thunderstorms produce strong winds. These are not tornadoes—they are called *straight-line winds*. Wind speeds can exceed 100 mph. These are often referred to as *downbursts* or *microbursts*.

## Dr. Ed, GOLFER

**I was playing golf during a thunderstorm one...**

**Oh, never mind.**

## Highs & Lows

**Hailstones weighing more than 2 pounds each fell in the Gopalganj district of Bangladesh on April 14, 1986. These hailstones killed 92 people and are the heaviest hailstones ever recorded.**

**4-inch diameter hailstone**

**Trees blown down during a downburst**

# Storm in a Lasagna Pan

**Convection** is the action of warm air rising and cold air sinking. This simple movement of liquids and gases not only causes winds, but also storms. Here's a fun way to watch how a storm forms from the comfort of your own home.

## WHAT YOU NEED

Ice cube trays

Water

Blue food coloring

Use of a freezer

Lasagna pan

Water

Thermometer

Red food coloring

Use of a stovetop (optional)

Parent to help (if you use the stovetop)

## WHAT YOU DO

**1** Fill the ice cube trays with water and add a drop or two of blue food dye to each cube. Put the ice cube trays in the freezer and leave them overnight.

**2** Fill the lasagna pan about three-quarters full with water, and let the water sit until it is room temperature.

**3** Gently place a blue ice cube in the pan at one end. Try not to disturb the water.

**4** Add a few drops of red food coloring to the water at the other end of the pan. Once again, try not to disturb the water. The cold blue water sinks while the warm red water rises. The blue water "cold air mass" pushes the unstable red water "warm air mass" upward. So, in weather terms, as the warm air is lifted by the cold air, the air cools. The air condenses and cumulus clouds can form. Condensation high up in the cloud falls to the ground.

**5** If you have a parent nearby who can help, you can try this using a stovetop. Wash out the pan and fill it once again about three-quarters full with room-temperature water. Place one end of the pan over a burner on the stove. This is where a parent's help comes in. Turn the burner on low and add a couple of drops of red food coloring to the cool end of the pan. The red water (cool water) will move toward the warm end. Then it will rise upward and back to the cool end. This is called a convection current. The same thing happens in the atmosphere when a storm is forming.

## Highs & Lows

**Tororo, Uganda, has thunder more often than any other place on Earth. It averaged 251 days of thunder per year for more than nine years.**

# Tornadoes

Tornadoes are the worst storms around. The strongest tornadoes can have wind speeds approaching 300 mph and can flatten just about everything in their path. The good news? Most tornadoes aren't nearly this strong. And even most of the really strong ones are less than 1 mile wide. So, the odds of being smushed by a tornado are really very small.

What is a tornado, then? It's a rapidly spinning column of air that forms between the bottom of a storm cloud and the ground. Air is invisible. Can you imagine if tornadoes were invisible? SCARY! Fortunately, tornadoes pick up a lot of dirt and stuff and, with water droplets forming in the funnel, they become visible. Tornadoes are also low-pressure areas. Air rises in the middle of that funnel cloud. Things as large as trees can be uprooted and lifted hundreds of feet into the sky. Cars can become airborne, too. (It's the return to Earth that hurts.) Hey, tornadoes have even moved railroad cars.

## How Does a Tornado Form?

All significant tornadoes develop from thunderstorms. The stronger the thunderstorm, the more likely it is to produce tornadoes. Supercell thunderstorms are the worst. Remember the updraft in a thunderstorm (see page 99)? Under the right conditions, air pulled into the updraft from under the storm will start to spin. A tornado is formed. Fortunately, this doesn't happen that often. Only a small fraction of all thunderstorms produce tornadoes.

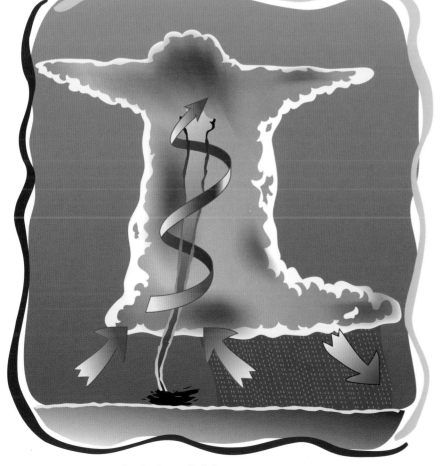

**A spinning updraft forms a tornado.**

**Tornado damage**

# Classifying Tornadoes

Meteorologists classify tornadoes according to how strong they are. They use the *Fujita*, or *F scale*, which was developed by Dr. Ted Fujita, a man who spent much of his life studying thunderstorms and tornadoes. Tornadoes range from minimal a F0 to an incredible F5. What's the difference between an F4 and a F5? Tornadoes can only be rated after they hit something. If your house were hit by an F4, you'd come home and say "Golly (or something worse), my house was hit by a tornado." If it were hit by an F5, you'd come home and say, "Where's my house?" Literally, it could be turned into splinters. By definition, an F5 tornado leaves only the bare foundation of the house. Fortunately, 75 percent of all tornadoes are F0 and F1, and less than 1 percent are F5.

| SCALE | WIND SPEED (MPH) | EXPECTED DAMAGE |
|-------|------------------|-----------------|
| F0 | 40–72 | Light |
| F1 | 73–112 | Moderate |
| F2 | 113–157 | Considerable |
| F3 | 158–206 | Severe |
| F4 | 207–260 | Devastation |
| F5 | 261–318 | Leveling |

**TRUE or FALSE**

A tornado can measure up to 5 miles in diameter.

**False.** The largest recorded tornado was nearly 1 mile in diameter. It struck near Mulhall, Oklahoma, in 1999, and measured 5,250 feet in diameter—which is just 30 feet shy of a mile.

# Tornado Facts

- "Tornado Alley" refers to an area of the United States stretching from central Texas to Nebraska. There are more tornadoes here than any place else in the world. But, tornadoes have occurred in each of the 50 states.

- Tornado season is in the spring. May and June have the most tornadoes. But (again), tornadoes can occur in any month.

- The worst rash of tornado activity occurred on April 3 and 4 in 1974. In a 24-hour period, 147 tornadoes were reported from Mississippi to New York. There were 24 F4 storms and six F5s. More than 300 people were killed.

- Officially, forecasts for tornadoes are similar to severe thunderstorms. The NWS issues a watch if conditions are favorable for tornado development. This means there's a threat of a tornado. NWS issues a warning if a tornado has been sighted or is indicated on radar. This means an tornado is in the area.

- Tornado watch areas are very large and most people within the area will never see a tornado.

- Doppler radars (see page 122) were specifically developed to detect severe thunderstorms and especially tornadoes. Since they became widely used in the 1990s, these radars have increased the lead time on tornado warnings, giving people more time to seek shelter.

- Besides tornadoes, we also have *water spouts* (usually weak tornadoes over water), *land spouts* and *gustnadoes* (weak tornadoes over land), and *dust devils* (weak swirls common in hot, dry areas).

- Check out these websites: **http://www.spc.noaa.gov** has tornado forecasts and reports as well as severe thunderstorm info; **http://www.tornadoproject.com** has extensive records on past tornadoes (my friend Tom Grazulis has spent much of his life collecting all this data).

## I DIDN'T KNOW THAT!

Storm chasers, such as those in the movie *Twister*, are really out there. Some do this for scientific research. Some do it for fun. It can be dangerous. Most storm chasers are experts who know what they're doing. They always approach a storm from the rear, where there is good visibility and the storm is moving away from them. (Okay, so those folks in *Twister* didn't do this, but that's a movie.) And, unlike the movies, most chases fail to "catch" a tornado.

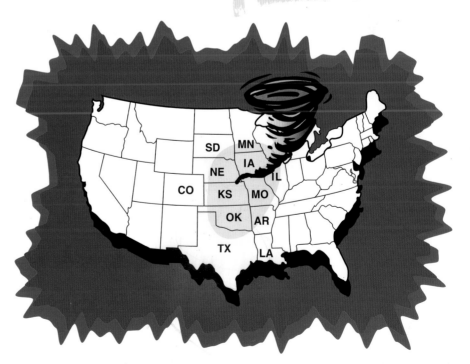

**Tornado alley**

# Hurricanes: Not Just a Lot of Wind

Hurricanes are technically called *tropical cyclones*. Cyclone means a low-pressure area and, in fact, the lowest pressures ever recorded near the Earth's surface have been in tropical cyclones. Tropical refers to where they form— near the equator and always over warm water. So, hurricanes are lows usually a few hundred miles across with showers and thunderstorms swirling around within the storm. Although not as strong as the strongest tornadoes in terms of wind speeds, the strongest hurricanes can have winds approaching 200 mph.

Another element common with these systems is rain—lots of rain. Rainfalls of 10 to 20 inches (or more) have occurred with many hurricanes. And they don't have to be strong to produce flooding rains. Allison in 2001 wasn't a hurricane, just a tropical storm, when it dropped

22-Sep   4:14

nearly 30 inches of rain in the area of Houston, Texas. Although Floyd was a significant hurricane when it came ashore in North Carolina in 1999, it was the rain, 15 to 20 inches, that produced the most damage.

**Before a hurricane**

**After a hurricane**

# Classifying Hurricanes

Like tornadoes, hurricanes are classified by their strength. Because hurricanes are larger and last longer, readings on pressure and wind speed are collected and used to classify the storms while they're still going on. The Saffir-Simpson scale ranks hurricanes from Category 1 to 5. On the average, the Atlantic Ocean has two storms that reach at least Category 3 status each year. One Category 4 storm occurs most years, but not always. Category 5 storms are, fortunately, rare, occurring about every four or five years.

## SAFFIR-SIMPSON SCALE

| CATEGORY | CENTRAL PRESSURE | | WINDS (mph) | SURGE (feet) | DAMAGE |
| --- | --- | --- | --- | --- | --- |
| | Mb. | Inches | | | |
| 1 | >980 | >28.94 | 74–95 | 4–5 | Minimal |
| 2 | 965–979 | 28.50–28.91 | 96–110 | 6–8 | Moderate |
| 3 | 945–964 | 27.91–28.47 | 111–130 | 9–12 | Extensive |
| 4 | 920–944 | 27.17–27.88 | 131–155 | 13–18 | Extreme |
| 5 | <920 | <27.17 | >155 | >18 | Catastrophic |

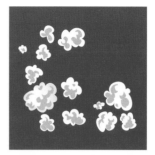

Several thunderstorms

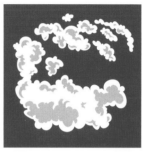

Tropical storm

Hurricane

# How Do Hurricanes Form?

A hurricane needs three basic ingredients: warm ocean waters, some of that Coriolis stuff (see page 67) to start a spin in the atmosphere, and weak winds in the upper level of the atmosphere to allow maximum thunderstorm development.

It also needs something to get it going: some type of initial disturbance. *Easterly* or *African waves* are low-pressure systems that move off the coast of Africa, to the west and all the way across the Atlantic Ocean in the summer. Some of these become hurricanes each year.

# Hurricane Facts

● Only three Category 5 storms have hit the United States since official records have been kept: the Labor Day storm that hit the Florida Keys in 1935; Camille, which came ashore in Gulfport, Mississippi, in 1969; and Andrew, which devastated southern Florida in 1992. Interestingly, Andrew was upgraded from a Category 4 to a 5 in 2002 based on a new analysis of the data recorded during the storm.

● The name "hurricane" is only used for storms in the Atlantic (this includes the Caribbean Sea and the Gulf of Mexico) and eastern Pacific Ocean. In the western Pacific, tropical cyclones are called typhoons. Near Australia, they're simply called cyclones.

● Hurricanes can't develop on or very near the equator. There is no Coriolis there to start the spinning motion.

● We have fewer hurricanes during El Niño years due to stronger winds high in the atmosphere. Winds are weaker with La Niñas, so we have more hurricanes.

● Tropical cyclones are classified by their wind speed as they develop or dissipate. A tropical depression has wind speeds of 30 to 40 mph. If winds exceed 40 mph, the system is called a tropical storm and is given a name by the folks at the National Hurricane Center (**http://www.nhc.noaa.gov**). Only when sustained winds are more than 72 mph is the system called a hurricane.

● You've probably heard weather people talk about "Hurricane Season." This is the time of year when most hurricanes form. Officially, it goes from June 1 through November 30. Most storms occur from the middle of August through September. Nature doesn't always follow our calendar though, and storms have occurred even in the colder months.

● How 'bout some averages? The Atlantic region averages 10 tropical storms a year, with six of these usually reaching hurricane force. About two storms per year hit the United States. Other parts of the world get tropical cyclones, too—about 80 per year.

**1** eye wall
**2** storm clouds
**3** eye
**4** spiraling winds
**5** hot air

# Inside a Hurricane

When I say hurricanes measure hundreds of miles across, I'm talking about the entire storm, not just the really strong part. Most of the outer layer of the storm consists of areas of showers and thunderstorms; these are the rain bands of the storm. Winds increase as you get closer to the center, but hurricane force winds are usually concentrated within 50 miles or less of the center. The heart of a hurricane is called the *eye wall*. This is a ring of thunderstorms that surrounds the center. The strongest winds and heaviest rains are found here. At the true center of the storm is the *eye*. Although the lowest pressures are found here, winds are light and calm and skies are often clear. If the eye of a hurricane moves

# Hurricane on the Move

Ever notice that hurricanes and other tropical systems move from east to west while they're still in the tropics? They're embedded in the easterly Trade Winds I talked about on page 65. When hurricanes move northward, they move into the Westerlies and turn to the north and east. Oftentimes it's fairly easy to forecast where a hurricane will go if the upper-level winds are strong. If the upper-level winds are weak, then hurricanes can move in any direction and even move in loops.

Hurricanes weaken quickly when they move over land. They are cut off from the warm ocean waters that "feed" them. Although winds die down quickly, heavy rains can persist for days. Storms also weaken over water if the water cools. Hurricanes also weaken if the upper-level winds become too strong and produce wind shear (page 66), which ruins the storm's structure. Occasionally, a hurricane will become just a common low just like the lows we get in winter.

over you, don't be fooled. The storm will start again shortly, with strong winds coming from a different direction than before. Eyes vary in size from 4 miles across to 30 miles or more.

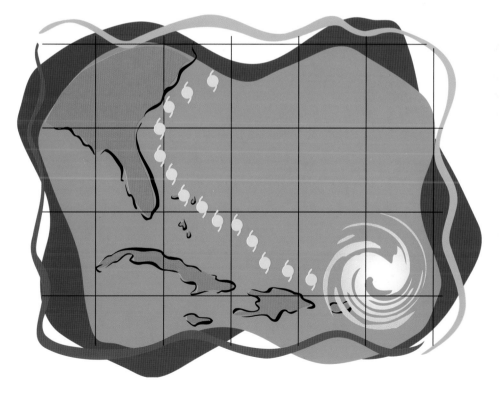

111

# Damage Caused by Hurricanes

About 20 people are killed each year by hurricanes in the U.S. More people die from bee stings. This is due to the excellent warnings sent out by the folks at the National Hurricane Center. Most people heed the warnings and leave coastal areas, where the threat is greatest. In other parts of the world, though, thousands of people are killed each year by tropical cyclones simply because they have no means of getting out of harm's way. In the U.S., the amount of damage caused by hurricanes is steadily increasing and is in the billions of dollars most years. You can't move your house out of the storm's path, and more and more people now live along the coasts.

What elements of a hurricane are the greatest hazards? Strong winds, obviously, can do a lot of damage. Hurricane Andrew in 1992 devastated south Florida with winds exceeding 150 mph.

Hundreds of houses were flattened. It was as if a massive tornado moved across the state. Speaking of tornadoes, hurricanes can produce them when they come ashore. Tornadoes can do more damage than the hurricane itself. Storm surges, the high tides that accompany a storm, can destroy a coastline. Hurricane Hugo in 1989 produced a 17-foot surge near Charleston, South Carolina. Hurricane Camille in 1969 (probably the strongest recorded storm to ever hit the US mainland) produced a tide 24 feet above normal in Gulfport, Mississippi. In recent years, the greatest threat from hurricanes hasn't been from strong winds, tornadoes, or storm surges, but rather from rain-produced floods. And these can occur well inland, away from where the storm comes ashore. It's estimated that 80 percent of the people who die in hurricanes in this country drown in freshwater floods.

**Here's a list of the most severe hurricanes and the damage they produced in the U.S.**

| | | |
|---|---|---|
| 1. Andrew | 1992 | $27 billion |
| 2. Hugo | 1989 | $9 billion |
| 3. Floyd | 1999 | $6 billion |
| 4. Georges | 1998 | $6 billion |
| 5. Allison | 2001 | $5 billion |
| 6. Fran | 1996 | $5 billion |
| 7. Isabel | 2003 | $4 billion |
| 8. Opal | 1995 | $3 billion |
| 9. Alicia | 1983 | $3 billion |

# Tracking Hurricanes

Casualties from hurricanes would be much worse were it not for the timely warnings issued by the National Hurricane Center in Miami, Florida. The meteorologists there track the storms by satellite when they first form. If they move closer to land, hurricane hunter planes are sent into the storm to get even more information. (It's a bumpy flight but not that dangerous for the experienced pilots.) If the storm approaches land, hurricane watches are issued to alert the public. Hurricane warnings may come later and these mean take cover or evacuate, if necessary. The storms are given names so the public has an easy way to identify them.

**A hurricane as seen from space**

## Dr. Ed ACTIVITY

# Become a Storm Tracker

**Use the tracking chart on page 127 to track the hurricanes and tropical storms that develop in a season.**

### WHAT YOU NEED
Tracking chart (page 127)
Pen or marker

### WHAT YOU DO

**1** When a tropical storm or hurricane forms, you can go to the NHC website (**www.nhc.noaa.gov**) to find out where it is at any given moment. Use the pen to log the coordinates given. Oftentimes, weather forecasters on television will give you the storm's longitude and latitude. (Latitude are the numbers that run along the left-hand side of the chart; Longitude are the numbers on the top of the chart.)

**2** When you figure out the coordinates of a storm, place a dot on the chart, and note the date and time. Check in again six hours later or so, and figure out the storm's new location. Do this as the storm develops, moves, and eventually dies out.

# CHAPTER 8

# Putting It All Together

**O**KAY, Weather Fanatics, it's time to put the whole weather puzzle together. A few more tidbits and you'll be amazing your family and friends with your ability to forecast the weather.

You figured out that we live at the bottom of an ocean of air called the atmosphere. And weather is what's going on there. Like a doctor who checks your temperature and blood pressure to see what's going on in your body, forecasters perform daily check-ups on the atmosphere and make predictions. They measure air pressure to see if it's high or low. They check the temperature to see if the air is hot or cold. They check the wind to see what direction the air is coming from and how fast it's moving. They measure the humidity to see how much water is in the air. And finally, they measure precipitation when it occurs. Guess what? You can do all that as well!

# Final Pieces to the Weather Puzzle

**You can't call yourself a weather forecaster until you know about weather systems, the real controllers of the weather. Read on, Weather Fanatics!**

## Air Masses

Highs are often associated with *air masses*, which are large masses of air (pretty good, huh?). These masses of air can be cold or warm, moist or dry. If air sits over a place for days or weeks, it takes on the characteristics of the area it is sitting over. For example, if an air mass is over northern Canada in the winter, it becomes very cold and dry. If an air mass sits over the tropical Atlantic Ocean in the summer, it becomes very warm and humid. Once these air masses start moving, they bring their weather with them. Winter cold spells in the lower 48 states are courtesy of Canadian air masses. The heat and humidity of the summer are courtesy of air from the tropics.

## Classifying Air Masses (Highs)

We can classify (we're doing that again) different air masses.

● Polar air is your typical cold air in winter. Polar air does occur in summer, but it doesn't get as far south and isn't nearly as cold as it is in winter.

● Even colder than polar air is Arctic air. This comes from closer to the North Pole and can bring record low temperatures, often below 0°F.

● On the other side, we have tropical air, the hot, sticky air mass so common in the summer. And yes, there is tropical air in winter. It doesn't get as far north as it does in summer and is mild, not warm during winter.

● Areas along the coasts can also be affected by marine air off the ocean. The actual temperature of the air depends on the water temperature. The cold current off California makes the marine air there very cool in the summer and is common in San Francisco. The warmer waters on the Atlantic side of the United States can make coastal temperatures there 20°F to 30°F warmer than inland locations in the winter.

## Low Pressure Systems

What about low pressure areas? Lows, which spin counterclockwise in the Northern Hemisphere, are the common storm systems in the winter. They bring rain or snow and often bring strong winds. Fortunately, they're smaller than highs and move faster, so, they usually bring bad weather for just a day or two. Lows are found between high pressure areas and usually between cold and warm air masses.

### Fronts

Cold air and warm air are separated by what we call *fronts*, which are usually found between two highs and are often associated with low pressure. Fronts often bring clouds and rain or snow. Sometimes when a front passes through, there are dramatic changes in the weather. The wind changes direction quickly and can become gusty. Temperatures may change abruptly.

### Classifying Fronts

There are different types of fronts.

● A ***cold front*** brings in colder air behind it. Often there are brief showers and thunderstorms ahead of the front. So, a cold front marks the end of the storm.

● A ***warm front*** brings in warmer air. Steady rain and fog are common before the front passes. Also, warm fronts mark the beginning of a storm.

● A ***stationary front*** (want to guess?) doesn't move much.

● An ***occluded front*** has little temperature difference on either side of it. It's usually associated with a strong low.

● Your barometer will drop as a front approaches and rise as the front moves past.

**Clouds forming at the front boundary of a cold front**

# What Causes the Weather? (A Review)

The Sun heats the Earth, but not evenly. The equator gets a lot more heating than the poles. The atmosphere then tries to move this extra heat from the tropics to the polar regions. This causes the air to move, producing wind. The atmosphere organizes itself into weather systems. It's these weather systems that do the work of moving the energy. These include jet streams, air masses, high and low pressure areas, and fronts. Sometimes the atmosphere goes into overdrive. That's when we get weather systems that can do damage—thunderstorms, tornadoes, and hurricanes.

Water tags along for the ride with the air. Water vapor (water in the form of a gas) is always in the air. When air is lifted, it cools, and the water vapor can condense forming clouds. If the lifting is strong, like it often is with lows and fronts, the clouds can produce precipitation. Eventually the water that falls from the sky will make it back into the air and the process starts again.

# Dr. Ed ACTIVITY

# Put Your Weather Station Together

**We've covered most of the important weather instruments and what they measure. You've had a chance to build your own instruments or go out and buy some. Now, you can put them all together to build a weather station.**

## WHAT YOU NEED

Barometer

Thermometer

Hair hydrometer
  or psychrometer

Rain gauge

Wind vane

Anemometer or Beaufort scale

## WHAT YOU DO

**1** The only instrument that can be used inside is the barometer. Air pressure is the same inside or out. So, just put the barometer where it's safe and easy to read.

**2** Your thermometer needs to be out of the sun during the day. One way to do this is to find a box or crate that air can flow through easily. Put it on its side and fasten the thermometer to the bottom, which is now up on its side. Then, place the box on a table or on some cinder blocks on the north side of your home or some other shady location.

**3** Your rain gauge needs to be in the open, well away from any buildings or trees that could block the rain or snow.

**4** Your wind vane and anemometer also need to be away from any buildings or trees that can block the wind. The higher up you can get them, the better.

**5** You can take outside humidity readings with either a psychrometer or hygrometer.

**6** Take your readings when it's a convenient time to do it. You need to be consistent and do it at the same time every day. Either in the morning before school or when you get home.

117

# Forecasting Considerations

Besides air pressure, temperature, wind, and precipitation, there are a few other things to consider when making a forecast.

## Your Climate

*Climate* is weather over a long period of time. It's the averages, extremes, and trends in the weather. It gives you reference points when looking at today's weather. What's the average temperature for today? What's the hottest and coldest it's ever been on this date? Has it been getting hotter or colder in recent years? The standard period of time for determining averages is 30 years. So, before you make your first forecast, know something about the place your forecasting for.

To check out past weather, go to **http://weather.gov**. On the map, click on your location. On the menu, find an item that says Past Weather or Climate and click on it. Find your hometown. Choose the month you're in now but the year before. Scroll down to your date today and see what the weather was like one year ago. (Newspapers & TV often have last year's weather, too.)

Although the weather is almost never "normal," average values for temperature will give you an idea of "ballpark" figures. Record highs and lows will give you reference points. If your forecast temperature would break a record, you may want to reconsider it. It's possible but unlikely.

## Your Current Weather

There's one simple rule to follow when forecasting the weather: what the weather is today may be the same weather as tomorrow. Today is your starting point. The first question to ask is, "Will tomorrow be different from today?" If not, then you can use today's weather to make tomorrow's forecast. This is called *persistence forecasting*. And, surprisingly enough, it works pretty well, especially when you're in a stretch of good weather. If you think tomorrow will be different from today, you must have a reason why. You need to have a picture in your head of what tomorrow will look like in terms of the weather. Then, you can make a forecast.

## Where You Live

Are you near any large bodies of water? What's your elevation? Do you live in a city, the suburbs, or in a more rural setting? Do more thorough climate research to see how where you live affects your forecast.

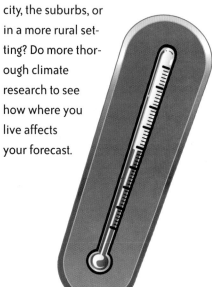

# You're a Forecaster Now

**Attention Weather Fanatics!  It's time to start making your own weather forecasts like the pros do!**

So, what's in a standard forecast? The first and most important thing is the actual weather conditions. Will it be fair or cloudy? Will there be precipitation? How much will fall and when will it occur? What type of precipitation will occur? Temperature comes next. Forecast the high and low for the next day. When will they occur? Keep track of your observations in your weather log.

## Forecasting Precipitation

● See how the air pressure is changing. Falling pressure indicates an approaching front. This usually brings rain or snow. Rising pressure indicates a high is moving in and the weather should improve. Often it means cooler temperatures too.

● Check the wind direction. Use the rules we learned in Chapter 4 to make a forecast.

● Determine if the humidity or dew-point has been changing recently. Increasing moisture means clouds and precipitation are likely. Decreasing moisture indicates clearing weather.

● Check out the cloud type. Use the table given in Chapter 6. Increasing cloud cover is a sure sign of moisture coming in. But you also need something to trigger the precipitation. An approaching front or low-pressure area often brings rain or snow. In the summer, strong heating during the day can trigger shower and thunderstorm formation.

● In the winter time, you may have to be concerned about forecasting precipitation type. Will it be rain, snow, freezing rain, or sleet? So, not only do you have to forecast the precipitation itself but also the temperature **exactly** if it will be near freezing.

● In the summer, you don't have to worry about what type of precipitation will fall. But forecasting rain in the summer is harder than in the winter. Winter weather makers such as big lows bring widespread areas of precipitation. So, it's pretty easy to know if it will rain or not. In the summer, showers and thunderstorms can be very localized. Check your local area to see if some places tend to get rain more often.

## Forecasting Temperature

● Do you expect any fronts to pass through? Warm fronts will bring warmer air while cold fronts will bring colder conditions.

● We said before low temperatures usually occur near sunrise and highs occur in the afternoon.

● The amount of cloud cover often has a major effect on temperatures. Clear skies allow the most heating during the day but also allow that heat to escape at night. Clear days usually have higher highs and lower lows—a greater range in temperatures. Cloud cover blocks sunlight during the day but holds in the Earth's heat at night. Cloudy days have a smaller range in temperature.

● Wind also affects temperatures. With fronts, it's the winds that bring in the colder or warmer air masses. North winds are usually cold while south winds are warm. Winds at night mix the air. On these nights, temperatures decrease with height and the ground doesn't get as cold. It's those calm, clear nights when surface temperatures can really fall.

● Keep in mind that precipitation can affect temperatures greatly. Some of that precipitation evaporates back into the air taking heat with it. Rain or snow always cools the air.

## Dr. Ed ACTIVITY

# Score Your Forecast

I use a scoring system for my students and have them compete against each other and against the computer forecasts. You get one point for each degree your high and low is off by. Precipitation we grade by yes or no. Add five points to your score if your precipitation forecast is incorrect.

Keep in mind, the lower the score, the better the forecast. Keep track of other forecasts too and see how you do against them. And don't worry about wrong forecasts. See if you can figure out what went wrong, and learn for the next time.

# Weather Maps

The weather map is one of the most important tools a meteorologist has. These maps show the "weather makers," and forecasters can use what we know about them to make a forecast. What do these maps show?

- High and low pressure systems
- Fronts
- Temperature
- Wind direction
- Precipitation

Check out this weather map. It's showing a possible winter situation. Match the number on the map with the description, using the key provided.

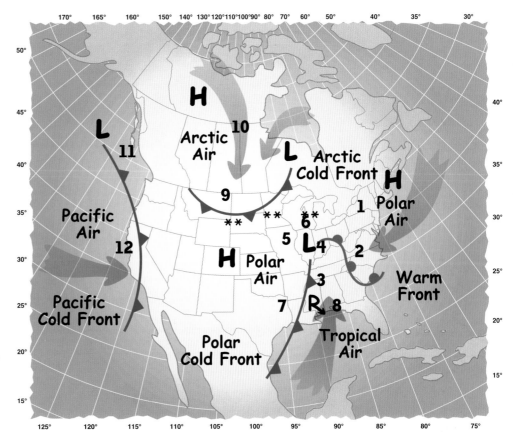

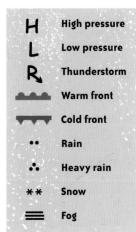

| | High pressure |
| H | |
| L | Low pressure |
| R | Thunderstorm |
| ▲▲▲ | Warm front |
| ▼▼▼ | Cold front |
| •• | Rain |
| •∴• | Heavy rain |
| ** | Snow |
| ≡ | Fog |

**1** Starting in the east, a polar high-pressure area is anchored in northern New England.

**2** The northeast flow around it has pushed the cold air all the way down to South Carolina.

**3** Further south and west, warm, tropical air is being pushed northward by strong southerly winds.

**4** A warm front separates the two contrasting air masses.

**5** A strong low pressure area south of Lake Michigan is pulling down cold polar air behind it with brisk northwest winds.

**6** Heavy snow is falling around Chicago.

**7** A cold front drops southward from the low separating the cold air to the west from the warm air to the east.

**8** Thunderstorms are occurring in the warm air ahead of the front.

**9** Just crossing into the northern Plains is an Arctic cold front. Snow showers precede it.

**10** Behind it, a strong high pressure area is dropping down from the Arctic regions.

**11** On the West Coast, a strong low in the Gulf of Alaska has whipped a cold front into the coast.

**12** The marine air behind the front is not that cold but the high elevations in the mountains support temperatures below freezing.

# The Forecaster's Best Friends

Without the following instruments, we might as well live in our ancestors' caves when it comes to forecasting!

## Weather Satellites

From where we stand here on Earth, all we can see are the bottoms of the clouds. But with the development of rockets and the space program, we now have another option. Cameras placed on satellites high above the Earth's surface can look down on the clouds and give us a perspective we never had before. And, so on April 1, 1960, the first weather satellite was launched, TIROS I. Today, images from weather satellites are shown on just about every weather show on television. Visible images use reflected sunlight during the day to show the clouds and the Earth. But at night, we can use the heat emitted from the clouds to still "see" them using infrared (heat) images.

## Radar

The police use radar guns to see how fast you're going. The military uses radar to see if enemy planes or missiles are coming. Meteorologists use radar to see precipitation. All radars use the same principle: they emit a pulse of energy (usually microwaves), and if there's an object out there, some of the

energy bounces back to a receiver. Then it can be displayed on a screen as an echo. When you see a weather radar display on TV, you're looking at rain or snow. If you track this area of precipitation over time, you can determine in what direction and at what speed it's moving. From that you can make a forecast. Radar can also determine how hard it's raining or snowing. When you see the different colors on a typical weather radar display, you're looking at different intensities of precipitation from light (usually green) to very heavy (usually red). Thunderstorms often have very large raindrops in them and show up well on radar. So, radar is a great tool for detecting thunderstorms (and all the severe weather that can come with them) and predicting their movement. Doppler radar is the big new thing. Without getting too technical, let's just say that a radar with Doppler can determine if areas of precipitation are moving towards or away from the radar set and how fast. Why is this so important? With Doppler, you can see rotation or spin in a thunderstorm. This is a good indication that the thunderstorm can be damaging or even produce tornadoes.

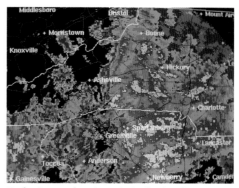

**Radar image showing rain in the Carolinas**

**Satellite image of Hurricane Emily**

**A Doppler radar**

**W**ELL, BUDDING WEATHER FANATICS, I'm just about done here. As my students like to point out, I am ENTHUSIASTIC about the weather. I hope you are, too. Even without the instruments and everything else, we can all stand outside and just enjoy the weather!

# Glossary

**absolute zero**. −450°F. The temperature at which atoms and molecules stop moving.

**air masses**. Large masses of air.

**air pressure**. The weight of air.

**anemometer**. Instrument used to measure wind speed.

**astraphobia**. Fear of lightning.

**atmosphere**. The air around you.

**atmospheric pressure**. Air pressure.

**autumnal equinox**. The first day of fall for the Northern Hemisphere, on or around September 23. See also equinox.

**ball lightning**. Continuous electrical discharge in the form of a glowing ball.

**barometer**. Instrument used to measure air pressure.

**Beaufort Scale**. Classification system for wind speed, with a range from 0 (calm) to 12 and above (hurricane-force).

**bow echo**. Thunderstorm in the middle of a squall line.

**brontophobia**. Fear of thunder.

**cloud**. Mass of cooled air.

**cold air drainage**. The tendency for cold air to sink to the lowest point if there is no wind.

**cooling degree day**. Energy industry term to indicate the day's temperature was above 65 °F.

**convection current**. The transfer of heat by upward air motion.

**coriolis**. Weather element that causes high pressure systems to spin clockwise and low pressure systems to spin counter-clockwise.

**crepuscular rays**. Sunlight made visible by clouds.

**cyclone**. Stormy weather caused by the rapid inward circulation of air masses about a low-pressure center.

**degassing**. The cooling of the Earth's crust soon after its formation.

**dew**. Water condensation, often on the ground.

**dewpoint**. Temperature at which air can become saturated with water vapor.

**dust devils**. Weak swirls of air common in hot, dry areas.

**El Niño**. A warming of the ocean surface off the western coast of South America that creates unusual weather patterns.

**equinox**. When a day and night are exactly the same length (12 hours) all over the world.

**evaporation**. The change of a liquid to a gas.

**eye**. True center of a storm.

**eye wall**. Heart of a hurricane, with a ring of thunderstorms that surrounds the center.

**flash floods**. Rapidly developing floods in streams and small rivers.

**fog**. Layer of cooled, saturated air near the ground.

# Glossary, *continued*

**frost.** Frozen water condensation.

**greenhouse effect.** The trapping of solar radiation and gases within the Earth's atmosphere.

**gustnadoes.** Weak tornadoes over land.

**halo.** Bright ring around the Sun or Moon.

**heat index.** Description of how the temperature feels based on a combination of temperature and humidity.

**heating degree day.** Energy industry term to indicate the day's temperature was below 65°F.

**heat lightning.** Colorful flashes of electrical energy in the sky, caused by a distant thunderstorm.

**hecta Pascal (hPa).** Unit of measurement. Also called millibar.

**humidity.** Water vapor in the air.

**hurricane.** A severe tropical cyclone that originates over the ocean near the equator.

**hygrometer.** Instrument used to measure humidity.

**inversion.** The tendency for calm, clear nights to cause the temperature on the ground to drop more than the temperature at higher elevations.

**jet stream.** River of air in the atmosphere approximately 5 miles above the earth's surface.

**knots.** Nautical miles per hour. One knot equals 1.15 mph.

**land spouts.** Weak tornadoes over land.

**La Niña.** A cooling of the ocean surface off the western coast of South America that affects weather patterns.

**lightning.** Electrical discharge in the atmosphere.

**meteorology.** The study of weather.

**meteorologist.** Person who studies weather.

**mesosphere.** The layer of atmosphere 30–50 miles above the surface of the Earth.

**millibar.** Unit of measurement. Also called hecta Pascal.

**persistence forecasting.** Basing forecasts on the most recent recorded weather.

**positive giant.** Lightning bolt that comes from the top of a cloud.

**pound per square inch (psi).** Unit of measurement.

**precipitation.** Water that falls from a cloud.

**psychrometer.** Instrument used to measure relative humidity.

**radiosondes.** Weather instruments that are attached to balloons and sent into the atmosphere to collect data.

**rainbow.** Arc of color on a curtain of rain droplets.

**rain gauge.** Instrument for measuring rainfall.

**relative humidity.** The amount of water vapor in the air compared to how much water the air could hold.

**saturation.** The point at which a substance can't hold any more liquid.

**sea breeze.** An onshore wind at a coast that usually develops during the warmest part of the day.

**seasonal affective disorder.** State of emotional and/or physical distress caused by lack of sunlight.

**severe thunderstorm.** Storm with strong winds, large hail, or tornadoes.

**solar radiation.** The warming rays of the Sun.

**specific heat.** The amount of energy required to raise the temperature of a substance by 1°C.

**squall line.** Line of thunderstorms.

**straight-line winds.** Strong winds produced by thunderstorms. Also called downbursts or microbursts.

**stratosphere.** The layer of atmosphere that contains Earth's ozone layer.

**storm surges.** Destructive high tides that accompany a storm.

**summer solstice.** The day each year when the Sun is at its highest and its rays are strongest, because the Northern Hemisphere is tilts the maximum toward the Sun, usually on or around June 21.

**sundogs.** Bright spots on either or both sides of the Sun.

**supercell.** A severe thunderstorm.

**thermometer.** Instrument used to measure temperature.

**thermosphere.** The top layer of Earth's atmosphere.

**thunder.** Sound made when a lightning bolt heats the air and the air expands quickly.

**tornado.** Weather system occurring over land, characterized by strong winds.

**trade winds.** Type of large-scale wind system.

**tropical depression.** Storm with wind speeds of 30 to 40 mph that forms over water.

**tropical storm.** Weather system with winds in excess of 40 mph.

**troposphere.** The layer of atmosphere nearest the surface of the Earth.

**updraft.** The rising air in the core of a cloud, often moving at nearly 100 mph.

**urban heat island.** Areas of concrete and asphalt, usually found in cities, that tend to absorb and retain solar radiation.

**vernal equinox.** The first day of spring for the Northern Hemisphere, on or around March 23. See also equinox.

**water cycle.** The process when water evaporate, condenses, falls as precipitation, then repeats the cycle.

**water spouts.** Weak tornadoes over water.

**water vapor.** Water in the form of gas.

**weather log.** A notebook for recording weather data.

**westerlies.** Type of large-scale wind system.

**wind.** Air in motion.

**wind chill factor.** A measurement of what it "feels like" that adds together the actual temperature and the cooling effect of the wind.

**wind shear.** Sudden change in wind speed or direction.

**wind vane.** Instrument used to measure wind direction.

**winter solstice.** The day each year when the Sun is at its lowest and its rays are weakest, because the Northern Hemisphere is tilted the maximum away from the Sun, usually on or around December 21.

# "Weather Information Everywhere" Chart

see page 14

| Source | High/low temperature predicted (°F) | Humidity (%) | Precipitation (type/inches) | Air pressure (mB) | Wind speed (mph) | Wind direction | Wind chill |
|---|---|---|---|---|---|---|---|
| Local TV news | | | | | | | |
| Local newspaper | | | | | | | |
| National internet weather site | | | | | | | |
| Radio | | | | | | | |
| National weather cable station | | | | | | | |

# Metric Conversion Chart

¼ inch = 6 mm
½ inch = 1.3 cm
¾ inch = 1.9 cm
1 inch = 2.5 cm
1½ inches = 3.8 cm
2 inches = 5.1 cm
2½ inches = 6.4 cm
3 inches = 7.6 cm
3½ inches = 8.9 cm
4 inches = 10.2 cm
4½ inches = 11.4 cm
5 inches = 12.7 cm
10 inches = 25.4 cm
12 inches = 30.5 cm
36 inches = 91.4 cm

To convert degrees **Fahrenheit** to degrees **Celsius**, subtract 32 and then multiply by .56. (Also, see page 43.)

To convert **inches** to **centimeters**, multiply by 2.5.

To convert **feet** to **centimeters**, multiply by 30.

To convert **feet** to **meters**, multiply by 30 and divide by 100.

To convert **miles** to **kilometers**, multiply by 1.6.

To convert **ounces** to **grams**, multiply by 28.

To convert **teaspoons** to **milliliters**, multiply by 5.

To convert **tablespoons** to **milliliters**, multiply by 15.

To convert **fluid ounces** to **milliliters**, multiply by 30.

To convert **cups** to **liters**, multiply by .24.

# Psychrometer Chart

see page 79

| Wet Bulb Reading (°F) | Dry Bulb Reading (°F) | | | | |
|---|---|---|---|---|---|
| | 60 | 65 | 70 | 75 | 80 |
| 45 | 22 | 12 | 3 | - | - |
| 50 | 44 | 31 | 19 | 9 | 3 |
| 55 | 68 | 52 | 36 | 24 | 13 |
| 60 | 94 | 75 | 55 | 40 | 29 |
| 65 | - | 100 | 77 | 58 | 44 |
| 70 | - | - | 100 | 78 | 61 |
| 75 | - | - | - | 100 | 79 |
| 80 | - | - | - | - | 100 |

# Weather Log Chart

see page 20

## LOG CHART

| Date | Conditions | Temperature | Barometric pressure | Wind direction | Wind speed | Wind chill | Relative humidity | Dew point | Cloud cover | How weather changed during the day | My prediction for tomorrow | Was I correct? Why? Why not? |
|------|-----------|-------------|---------------------|----------------|-----------|-----------|-------------------|-----------|-------------|-----------------------------------|---------------------------|------------------------------|
|  |  |  |  |  |  |  |  |  |  |  |  |  |
|  |  |  |  |  |  |  |  |  |  |  |  |  |
|  |  |  |  |  |  |  |  |  |  |  |  |  |
|  |  |  |  |  |  |  |  |  |  |  |  |  |
|  |  |  |  |  |  |  |  |  |  |  |  |  |
|  |  |  |  |  |  |  |  |  |  |  |  |  |
|  |  |  |  |  |  |  |  |  |  |  |  |  |